an absorbing errand

an absorbing errand

HOW ARTISTS
and
CRAFTSMEN MAKE THEIR WAY
to
mastery

———

JANNA MALAMUD SMITH

COUNTERPOINT
BERKELEY

Library of Congress Cataloging-in-Publication Data is available.

ISBN 978-1-61902-004-7

Interior design by meganjonesdesign.com
Cover design by Natalya Bolnova

Printed in the United States of America

COUNTERPOINT
1919 Fifth Street
Berkeley, CA 94710
www.counterpointpress.com

Distributed by Publishers Group West

10 9 8 7 6 5 4 3 2 1

For Jack Beinashowitz, Alfred Margulies,
Humphrey Morris, and Stephen Sternbach,
stalwart readers and fellow travelers.

Les vrais paradis sont les paradis qu'on a perdus.
(The true paradises are those which we have lost.)

—MARCEL PROUST

CHAPTER 1

an absorbing errand

I

MY MOTHER-IN-LAW, EDITH Smith, was an even-tempered woman, except in late winter when cabin fever sometimes undid her and her quiet good nature would become quietly irritable. She was hardly alone among New Englanders who become blah in February; but unlike many others, her cure required neither travel to southern climes nor Prozac (though I mistakenly suggested the latter more than once). As soon as the March sun pried the worst of the snow crust off her garden, and the ground gave quarter to a shovel blade, she was cured. She would grab any old jacket and gloves, and out she'd go—hauling fallen branches, raking away mucky leaves, uncovering flower beds in time to reveal the first white snowdrops and the yellow winter aconite poking up from the icy ground. A monarch reunited with her realm, she felt palpable relief at resuming her proper duties. Though their unworldly green had yet to emerge from the clotted mud, she knew where her subjects resided, and she'd plan: how best to impede the poppies, when to separate the irises, and whether, finally, to trim back the aging, overgrown purple lilacs or simply let them sprawl. (She tended to indulge the lilacs.) The winter's apathy was vanquished.

Completely revitalized, she returned to herself. At ninety, over her daughter's ever-louder protests, she mowed her lawn in the summer heat or bent on her padded "kneeler" to yank weeds from among her flowers, conceding only to a hat against the steamy sun. Each time we visited, she'd modestly lead us among the beds. We might see primroses, crocuses, coral bells, peonies, tulips, and narcissus in spring; then coreopsis, bee balm, day lilies, daisies, and hollyhocks in midsummer; and finally, in early autumn, clumps of asters, sedum, chrysanthemums, and the last of the deep pink cone flowers. She encouraged our attention toward whatever bloomed and then protested our kudos. Our appreciation simultaneously confirmed her and yet reminded her of the next permutation already in mind, the way her worldly acre had further distance to travel before it might approach her ideal. Meanwhile, she'd offer us pots in which to carry away phlox, or black-eyed Susan, or whatever we'd admired. When, not long after she died, my husband and I moved to a new home, he dug up a clump of Solomon's seal she'd given us years before. It was his way of keeping her with him. Now, each April, he stands over the plant's dried, clipped autumn stalks, rake in hand, worrying new life out of the ground, relieved only when the shoots, exotic nematodes from the deep, poke up for another season.

THE GOOD LIFE is lived best by those with gardens—a truth that was already a gnarled old vine in ancient Rome, but a sturdy one that still bears fruit. I don't mean one must garden qua garden (I am myself desultory in that regard, gung ho in May but disinclined in sticky summer. When serious gardeners don their straw hats, I retreat to our dark, cool library). I mean rather the moral equivalent of a garden—the virtual garden. I posit that life is better when you possess a sustaining practice that holds your desire, demands your attention, and requires effort; a plot of ground that gratifies the wish to labor and create—and, by so doing, to rule over an imagined world of your own.

I grew up surrounded by writers, painters, potters, musicians—artists of all sorts. But it wasn't until I observed Edie in and out of her garden that the penny dropped, and I recognized the shared psychological patterns of all I had long witnessed. As with the literal act of gardening, pursuing any practice seriously is a generative, hardy way to live in the world. You are in charge (as much as we can ever pretend to be—sometimes like a sea captain hugging the rail in a hurricane); you plan; you design; you labor; you struggle. And your reward is that in some seasons you create a gratifying bounty.

Can gardening be talked about in the same breath with Art? I imagine a spectrum of creative artistic effort that stretches from serious craft to the most abstract, accomplished art. Arguably, its common elements include the wish to express oneself, and to move people deeply. I know that's a claim that stirs up more than it settles. Do Picasso's *Demoiselles* or Richard Serra's *Torqued Ellipses* really belong in the same sentence with the effect of grape hyacinth planted next to yellow species tulips? To make the comparison fairer, shouldn't Olmsted's Central Park be construed as an artistic creation on a par with many a great painting or sculpture? Or must the park await that label until after Christo and Jeanne-Claude have hung their orange curtains across its acreage? Yes, craft is more about utility and continuity. Miriam Leonardi, a chef at Zibello in Italy, explains, "I am not creative . . . That's not what I do. What I do is what has been handed down to me. For ten generations, maybe longer."[1] And art is more about originality, provocation, and comment; yet they often merge into each other, and they certainly share common elements.

My wish here is not to argue definitions (high art/low art/ craft, etc.) but rather to suggest that for a range of diverse "artistic" undertakings there exist *common* mental processes of mastery. One must work hard to learn technique and form, and equally hard to learn how to bear the angst of creativity itself. Furthermore, and also in common, the effort brings with it a whole herd of psychological obstacles—rather like a wooly mass of obdurate sheep settled on the road blocking your car. For you to move forward, these creatures must be outwitted, dispersed, befriended, or herded, their impeding genius somehow overcome or co-opted. Otherwise the would-be art-maker gives up on the outing without accruing enough skill, without staying with the effort long enough, to build a body of work and/or gain her own or a public's esteem. These sheep are my subject.

Perhaps you want to work at creating something challenging (something that may require a commitment of years for you to become technically adept, and that may often seem dreadfully difficult) like poems, ceramics, sculptures, photographs, paintings, performance art, or woven tapestries. But you find yourself putting off the attempt, or quitting as soon as you start, or midway through deciding you are talentless and it's useless to try, or if you are actually working, feeling intermittently too discouraged and too alone. What is happening? Well, you may be asking the wrong questions or placing mistaken expectations on yourself. Particularly, you may be unaware of how the necessary struggles of your own unconscious mind, if misunderstood, will bruise your heart, arrest your efforts prematurely, and prevent your staying absorbed in your errand. Yet, the same struggles, appreciated, will enable your creativity and the larger processes of mastery.

II

EDIE WAS HAPPY in her garden. Not inevitably, not always, but mostly. And I have declared that the labor of mastery may be a route to happiness. In truth, my own experience has been that writing also makes me dyspeptic and dispirited. The desired words do not come. In their place descends a damp malaise. I resist sitting still. I bemoan my incompetence. Any other endeavor feels more attractive than concentrating: unloading the dishwasher, plucking dead leaves off houseplants, deleting emails. Many people have told me about losing all sense of time as they focus on their work, settling into the task then "coming to" several hours later, unaware that the sun has crossed the yardarm. I envy them; I simply do not concentrate that deeply. (I call my sorry state "mother's mind"—always aware of my surroundings, tuned to a toddler's murmur, though my sons are grown, and my husband reminds me I was like this before they were born.) Moment by moment, for me, writing cannot predictably be conceived of as bliss.

So what's my claim? Well, if I mostly stay in my chair for half the morning, or several half mornings in a row, or many; if I resist enough of the temptations meant to distract me from the anxiety of the effort, then I often find my way through the soul's dreary sleet into something better. Like a recalcitrant mule that's resigned itself to haul a plow, my brain and body settle into the work. Better words rise, a richer soil from beneath the dull surface. (Years ago a poet friend entitled a collection *Listeners at the Breathing Place*—referring to an Eskimo lithograph of a hunter poised beside a hole in the ice where seals surface to breathe. A seal hunter waits, sometimes from before dawn until evening; he must settle within himself enough to survive the cold, and yet he must listen; he must remain alert, poised to throw a spear, to seize the fleeting opportunity—the brief surfacing flash of a needed word, or image, or musical note.)[2]

On such days, I end the morning's work feeling purposeful, grounded, even confirmed in some inchoate sense that, although I will suffer my portion of disappointment, grief, ill health, busywork, and commuter traffic, I am indeed living the life I want to live. My days feel meaning-filled and vivid. I am not just the woman inching the car forward; I am the seal hunter. This slight recasting of self is an essential aspect of our liberty. We control little, but through our choices of where we put our effort, we can inflect our idea of ourselves in small but crucial ways.

Lots of moments in any week, many of them random and hilarious, please me—especially when people dear to me are present. Yet, when they go well, each of the crafts I have attempted to master—writing, photography, and also psychotherapy—leaves me with a deep private sense of satisfaction. I feel stimulated, warm, slightly elated, or otherwise moved; content; purposeful. Though I don't think about it consciously, I sense I'm comfortably aligned with my ideal of myself. But there's more to it. Whether by design or by accident, many of us seem to find enduring gratification in struggling to master and then repeatedly applying some difficult skill that allows us at once to realize and express ourselves.

Even when separated from art-making, such work—in this case the sustained, and sustaining, *organic* relationship of person to process—captures our attention and our effort; it creates for us a particular privacy and with it an unforeseen and contradictory freedom. There's an evocative description at the beginning of Edward Jones's novel *The Known World*, of Moses, the enslaved overseer of slaves, tasting the plantation's dirt:

> *He ate it not only to discover the strengths and weaknesses of the field, but because the eating of it tied him to the only thing in his small world that meant almost as much as his own life . . . This was July, and July dirt tasted even more like sweetened metal than the dirt of June or May.*[3]

THE FREEDOM THAT slavery cannot entirely strip away is Moses's pleasure in his own knowledge, his sense of authority and the ensuing satisfaction—of having long studied the soil and, therefore, knowing its intimate mix of elements, what it can best grow, its readiness to be plowed or planted. The knowledge, like most knowledge, has public consequence, but its initial locus is private, and much of its pleasure remains private. The feelings and purposes around art-making, too, ricochet among private, public, and communal places, but the creative process often demands seclusion to germinate its seed.

By "organic" work I mean something close to *Merriam-Webster*'s "developing in the manner of a living animal." No machine blades sheer off minute from minute. No PowerPoint slide dictates the task at hand. The work grows as our minds (conscious and unconscious) and our bodies would have it grow. Technique may require discipline and set the order of things, apprenticeships may demand periods of subordination, but the imaginative acts that propel the effort are themselves serendipitous. In your garden you may set out to clip the roses, but you notice a weed you want to pull from among the coreopsis, except that first there is a rogue branch to be snipped from the holly shrub—and on and on until dark finally settles, ending your day. An occasional task has to be done just now and just so. But mostly, you delight in meandering, allowing the work to command your attention variously—with its method inscribed by the way you encounter your plants.

Such work guards a quality of timelessness within an ever-more-time-bound world. When Moses tastes the dirt, the action takes an instant, and yet it takes as much time as sensation requires. Time emerges from the activity rather than being imposed by the clock. As I write, there's the clock on my computer, the watch on my wrist, the clock on my desk, the clock on my telephone, the clock on my fax . . . each declaring the passing of a slightly different moment. Yet even I, who track the hours closely, understand that one pleasure of art-making is its resolute inefficiency. It resists the sweep of the second hand; it is opposite to my daily muster of punch lists, telephone calls, day job requirements, family life, and errands. The necessary thought may come today or next week. Yet it's not the same as leisure. The struggle toward that next thought is rigorous, held within an isometric tension. The poet Richard Wilbur writes about laundry drying on the line, "moving and staying like white water."[4] Moving and staying. Such water, familiar to anyone who has watched a brook rush over rocks, captures the way a creative practice insists you bear time. You must hold still and wait, and yet you must push forward.

And while one can complete a particular project, the labor itself is never finished, the mastery never final. I suspect its incompleteness, by turns fetching and vexing, is its consummate quality, its essence. I remember reading years ago that it takes about a decade to master a craft. Since then, many numbers have been bandied about, and the idea seems overdiscussed and a little silly. Still, ten years rings true to my own experience. Half a decade to begin to set your foot firmly. Yet even mastery so described is merely a breather snatched at an overlook on a long hike—a quick snapshot, a sip of water, and a retying of loose laces. But not an arrival. There is always the expanse yet to come—more to traverse, learn, do. There is always another variation to sample. After more than thirty years of practicing psychotherapy, I am still studying techniques and learning new approaches; it's the same with writing.

I remember an art student in Italy some decades ago describing to me the way the Renaissance fresco painters began their careers with long studio apprenticeships during which they practiced over and over the standard motifs—the receding tiled floor, the draped cloth, the winged angels, the arches and umbrella pines, the blue hills. When at last the hour came to brush pigment permanently onto wet plaster, not only did they have the outline of the sketch to follow, but also they had been well trained to quickly replicate the much-practiced motifs. The beauty of the particular fresco rested on the portraiture, the colors, and the rearranging of a scene; on the infinite variation made possible by compounding the more familiar details. What's more, new combinations could be pursued as long as there were walls and commissions.

Because the point of arrival is enigmatic, elusive, receding, because it wavers like a mirage on the road, always before us and only briefly with us, devoting oneself to mastering a practice unexpectedly leads through a time warp where past, present, and future commingle. I find the contradictory notion comforting. Contemporary life is all excerpts, fragments, reversals, and interruptions; it offends and delights us with its astounding, noisy discontinuity, but the work of mastery is very much as it was when artists thousands of years ago carved Cycladic figures or cast the Benin gold.

We know reality is constructed and mediated by our senses. But this work of mastery glorifies that labor of transcribing— of transforming perception from the invisible into the material world—so it can then become part of another person's experience. And *that* process leads us toward a singular human communion where proximity is created by continuity, shared emotions, and the resulting moments of recognition.

Visiting the Metropolitan Museum, I am drawn to an ancient Egyptian wood encaustic (an image produced by fixing wax colors with fire) painted in the second century called *Portrait of the Boy Eutyches*. I am dumbstruck by the child's appeal. His brown eyes are large, bright, and direct; his skin is smooth; his lacy white shirt offers contrast to his light olive skin; his full lips lift slightly into a winsome half smile, as if he gently seeks the artist's approval or shyly offers reassurance to him—and beyond him, to us. Someone really loved this boy. I am certain of it. He invites love in the way one does when one has been loved. Looking at him evokes fond memories of my own sons as young boys. Clock time is breached simultaneously on two fronts. I imagine his context in Egypt—the historic past—as alien and distant, a long time ago. And yet I feel a sense of its immediacy—here right now. So, too, an earlier era of my own family life returns sharply. The memory evoked by the painting overlays the picture. I could have been his mother; he could have been my son. What's more, when I think to write about the encaustic—or if a photographer seeks to record the same expression on a living face, or if a painter places the boy in a painting of his own, or a weaver finds inspiration in the child's shirt—a third relationship emerges, where the later effort reaches back and reinvigorates the dead artist's perspective and at the same time animates the contemporary work.

When we think about imaginative acts, we often only partially attend to their central, obvious power: the way they dissipate clock time, a breeze shooing off a fog, and thus the way they amend mortal loss. Edie is some years dead now, and yet she labors in her garden. My words, capturing her actions, mark and realize her surroundings, a free space where we may visit, linger, and recall. Our common creative labors restore older, more familiar rhythms of humanity, and by doing so they ground us and temper the particular fragmentation and disconnections that define our age.

III

OF MY OWN practices, writing most fully gratifies my need for self-expression. While a psychotherapist's method carries her own signature and is rooted within her sensibility, it is a relational practice. And, as with most efforts at supporting emotional growth, it focuses on putting others first. The place of technique, as well as the purpose of self-expression, is to allow the therapist to give mindful care. In 2002, a French documentary produced by Nicolas Philibert called *Être et Avoir* (*To Be and to Have*) profiled a teacher and his young students in a one-room schoolhouse in rural France. Reviewing the movie in *The New Yorker*, David Denby wrote about the teacher, Georges Lopez: "Watching the intensity of his work from moment to moment, child by child, is a demonstration of craft exercised on a level at which skill and love have become indistinguishable."[5] In a sense, the skill of the psychotherapist is to be able to deliver the elements of love to a patient in a tolerable fashion, so that the patient can take them in and metabolize them. Psychological growth is difficult, at some junctures impossible, without another person who provides aspects of love—love as nonjudgmental attention, love as careful listening and the effort to comprehend, love as courage and empathy, love as encouragement, love as struggle and challenge, love as meaning-making—though almost never are declarations of love helpful.

These same elements of love are relevant to art-making, and I reference them in later chapters. For now I want to focus on mastering a medium for the sake of self-expression, creativity, and/or producing objects of interest or beauty. In this sense, craft—or art-making—names the place where technique and hard work intersect both with the knowledge we've gathered and with whatever is unique about us—the particular way our minds, our thoughts, our perspective, and our feelings mix. The term "craftsman" in the past frequently emphasized anonymity, an ego subsumed within communal effort—a questionable truism but one oft repeated. (I sometimes wonder if they were truly anonymous, or whether the people who carved the cathedral stone, and craftspeople generally, simply lived in small communities where others knew who they were without their having to advertise.) Still, a worker often sought some measure of impersonal uniformity in his product: When members of a medieval guild built sets of chairs, one builder's chairs were meant to resemble another's closely enough to allow a set of six to contain the work of different men.

But craft, as I use the term, focuses particularly on a more individual ideal where the object is durably linked to one craftsman or creator. That's the thrill and the horror. If three woodworkers set about building three chairs, the finished products might all resemble one another, accidentally or by intention. Yet my meaning, shared by many since industrialization commenced, emphasizes the way, formed by different hands, each chair would bear distinctive marks. One person's style of choosing wood, lathing a leg, or planing an edge would likely be different from another's, and that variation would provide a locus for our pleasure. Given full rein, each woodworker's idea of a desirable chair would be her own. And each chair would emerge as the physical representation—the compromise between vision, technical capacity, materials, and market requirements—of the picture of a chair in her mind's eye: a solution that occurred to her, perhaps while she was seated in a chair that did not seem quite right to her. Occasionally, one such chair may be fresh or unsettling enough, or may somehow explore a larger meaning of "chair" enough, to be deemed a work of art.

Lewis Hyde, in his book *The Gift*, describes the creative moment as a gift we receive. Yet I often, more mundanely, experience it as if it were a funky badminton game, with shuttlecocks flying among different realms of the mind. Birdies arrive from nowhere, arced up into the air by an invisible hand. Our brain is many brains laboring at once, mostly outside of our awareness. From behind a scrim, something unseen strokes a racquet. Desire, patience, receptivity, hope, effort, and practice somehow create movement among neurons—not unlike the creation of dreams while we sleep or the found images elaborated in daydreams—but with a more active role for volition. By which I mean, though it is hard to pinpoint just how much and how, our own will does help to drive the strange mental progression that allows us to create something.

While the analogy I'm about to make is a cliché, I want to offer it anyway because it's visceral and apt and something I still feel sometimes: If you run some miles each week, however slowly and miserably, there comes a day when the air is clear, the humidity just right, when you suddenly float along effortlessly in an almost inconceivable lightness of being. Your muscles don't tire. You feel you could run and run. Often, no matter how much I may wish for the same lightness, the same ecstasy, on other days, it is nowhere to be found; I cannot will it. Yet even as it is beyond my summons, its singular appearance denotes a hard-won synthesis, an achievement, a complex integration of body and mind. The moment is the result, first and foremost, of steady running. The more days you exercise, the more opportunities you have to experience the "gift."

Similarly, serious singers know that parts of their voice are beyond their control. Involuntary systems produce or don't produce the timbre of a sound at a given moment or the perfect landing on the desired pitch. But singers also know that the more they practice and train, and sing, and actively imagine the desired sound, the more often the involuntary muscles and reflexes work as they need them to during a performance, and the more possibility there is for a transcendent moment in which everything comes together and their voices soar.

I am not certain why I feel uniquely satisfied when I write and itchy and not quite myself during hiatuses. Yet it is so. And when you find your work, you sense an altered discourse with your longing, and thus with yourself. We are, the philosopher and psychoanalyst Jonathan Lear reminds us, "finite erotic creatures."[6] I love this expression because it captures simply the haunting tension between our expansive desire and our knowledge of our inevitable death. Art is one way we bridge the two. Art holds and transmits some portion of our eroticism and our erotic energy. It deflects it from its primary aim and brings it into the world as creative expression. And it simultaneously defies death. I think of Audra McDonald singing "I Loves You, Porgy" in *Porgy and Bess*, conveying her helpless sexual terror, dependence, lust—her longing for safety and love. She knows life has slammed her, and will slam her again, yet she sings so your heart aches and your neck hairs stand on end. Like Bess, art announces, "Yes, I know the game is stacked. But I'll say my piece."

Mastering form so that it can capture energy, feeling gratified by the mastery, we find a way to bear our desire, to bear ourselves as finite erotic creatures. And what was before an aimless shouting into the night becomes a more particular conversation. It is as if a fundamental aloneness has been joined.

"I think of myself as writing for one person," Anne Sexton once observed, "that one perfect writer who understand[s] and loves."[7] Sort of. But really I mean, too, that a commitment to labor grants you a place at that rowdy seminar table in the sky. Greater voices dominate and carry on, but you have your chair, and no one stops you from sitting alert, craning and nodding, amid the buzz.

IV

I REMEMBER LOVING Studs Terkel's *Working* when it first came out in 1972. Thirty-five-plus years later, I recall an image from the book of a woman who has spent her work life pressing clothes. The woman—as I see her—is absently smoothing the chair arm, just the way for so many years her hands and arms labored smoothing cloth before she pressed it.[8] We become the work to which we dedicate ourselves. I know that now, but I began to grasp it then, while reading Terkel. Sometimes the change is physical—the woman's muscle memory of pressing clothing, or Louis Armstrong's cheeks, over decades of trumpeting, gradually stretching out like thick balloons. Glass blowers' faces alter similarly. Great singers over years may develop puffed-out chests. The Rembrandt self-portrait in the Frick Collection museum is striking for the foregrounding of the painter's hands. No accident, but an artist's view of himself that emphasizes the anatomy critical to his authority.

For many of us, the transformations are less visible—even invisible. Yet they are no less explicit. We incise some patterns at the expense of others. A violinist's fingers know a host of incremental ways to apply pressure to a string. I, in turn, know how to look away momentarily from a patient to heighten her privacy while she figures out what she is beginning to feel, what she wants to say, and then how to look up and meet her eyes when she finds words for something she didn't previously comprehend. The focus with which I listen to patients often switches itself on reflexively when someone outside the office speaks frankly. The habit of listening so particularly is engrained after decades. I am careful not to carry the whole consulting room into my life, not to offer therapy abroad, and yet I approach the world informed by my knowledge as a psychotherapist. For better and worse, I explain a variety of situations to myself according to its lights. I have also been formed by books and the people who led me to them. This compiled knowledge now sits within my habit of seeking words to describe experience. When something moves me, I begin retelling the tale.

I remember a wrenching moment with my mother several years before she died. I had done some errands for her. She wanted to thank me somehow. Often I could not let her. I wanted to let her. Was I hungry? she wondered. She wheeled her wheelchair to the refrigerator and listed out its contents, offering me everything within it. Her desire, mine, our difficulty finding an easy way to be with each other, welled up and overwhelmed me with sadness, guilt, intense helpless love. When, weeks later, I described the moment to a literary friend, she observed, "You're writing it already." And she was correct. I turned both to friendship and my habit of seeking words as ways of taming the anguish.

Our chosen practices form our perspectives. I recall a conversation I had long ago with the director of my children's day-care center, then in her sixties, when she was about to take her first trip to Europe with her husband and a granddaughter. She had worked hard all her life, and what bits of money she had ever mustered she had immediately spent raising children, and then foster children, and then grandchildren. This was the first time that she and her husband could even think of travel. They chose to go to England. While she was excited, her husband, a carpenter, felt reluctant. He wasn't sure he wanted to go abroad, but she urged him on and he agreed. When they returned, I was curious how his trip had been. "So, how was it for Roger?" I asked. "It was mixed," his wife responded, "but he loved seeing the Christopher Wren churches. He couldn't get over the carpentry. He enjoyed minutely examining each one." Our interest and competencies create the focus for our gaze, stimulate our curiosity about variation, allow us to seek and find fruit in what is initially an obscure grove.

Buying and selling—"getting and spending," in Wordsworth's words—crowd our land with markets, our rivers with barges, our roads with trucks, and our skies with airplanes; we are a species of traders and procurers. Not long ago, when I went to get my hair cut, the only animated conversation in the salon during my half hour in the chair was a discussion about which Caribbean islands to visit in order to buy the best Louis Vuitton luggage. The woman in the seat next to mine, the hair colorist tending to her, and the female owner standing behind them were all expert. They knew the different styles of suitcase by name; they knew each store on St. Thomas. They compared plans for next year's buying trip. Traveling to buy sought-after objects is an honorable practice and as old as time. Making deals warms the blood. Great stuff makes good prey, and I've gone abroad and hauled back my share of loot, ceramic tiles and old cow bells being two perennial favorites. Still, listening to the women talk reminded me that another benefit of craft or art-making is that the challenge of mastery provides an additional reason to leave one's home territory.

By bearing the anxiety of departure, by not saying no to the voyage, we open ourselves to unforeseen possibilities—like the surprise of the Wren church. Writing about Sancho Panza and Don Quijote in *Mimesis*, Erich Auerbach observes, "If Don Quijote had not gone mad, he would not have left his house. And then Sancho too would have stayed home, and he could never have drawn from his innate being the things which—as we find in delighted amazement—were potentially contained in it."[9] The love of a practice, the effort of trying to master it, gives us a different portal through which to enter the world and, thus, another way both to see new places and to draw from our innate beings the things that are potentially contained within it.

Which, in a roundabout way, brings me to Henry James—from whom I've taken the title of this book. In James's novel *Roderick Hudson*, the character Rowland Mallet has a notion about happiness that sums up the case I'm making in this chapter. In an early scene, Mallet explains himself to his cousin:

> *"True happiness, we are told, consists in getting out of one's self; but the point is not only to get out—you must stay out; and to stay out you must have some absorbing errand . . . Do you know I sometimes think that I am a man of genius half-finished? The genius has been left out, the faculty of expression is wanting; but the need for expression remains, and I spend my days groping for the latch of a closed door."*[10]

IN TRUTH, THE particular proposition as Mallet utters it bodes badly, for *Roderick Hudson* is a cautionary tale about the perils of forsaking one's own work in order to promote and finance someone else's. Mallet is wealthy. Right before he departs Massachusetts for Italy, he meets Roderick Hudson, a young sculptor. Mallet decides that Hudson's genius is such that he will make him his special project. He will support Hudson, set him up in Rome, and guide him to realize his talent. The novel recounts how badly the plan goes awry. Hudson is weak and undisciplined. Mallet lacks self-knowledge and is overly certain of his own virtue. He becomes an illustration of the perils of living vicariously, of hoping to gratify oneself through another's effort and achievements. Yet the quotation conveys well the feeling of inchoate desire for finding your own right work.

By Mallet's account, true happiness rests on discovering and pursuing an absorbing errand that satisfies your need for expression and keeps your focus "outside" yourself. This quotation is at once literal and paradoxical. Art-makers and craftsmen are both exorbitantly inside and yet insistently, existentially, outside themselves. By going in, they go out. And vice versa. To feed the fire, they must gather kindling in deep woods. And while dragging back branches, often becoming tangled in the briers, they have the opportunity to listen and to look around. Thus Sancho Panza's awakening as he accompanies Don Quijote, or Roger's delight in the complexity of the joints and joists in the Wren churches. An absorbing errand is the agreement to undertake and sustain a compelling practice of your own, an effort at mastery that requires time and focus. It is an adventure with many perils. Yet, in return, you gain a window seat, forward motion, and a landscape made new.

fears

"I SPEND MY DAYS groping for the latch of a closed door," Rowland Mallet explains in *Roderick Hudson*, capturing the baffled sense we have before we find our right labor or, having found it, before we settle fully into the effort it demands or begin to master its techniques and discover its rhythms. Though perhaps keenest in early adulthood when life is ungelled in its mold and emotions run deep, such frustrations mark any beginning. You are fine, but you are not. You are quietly unsettled: nagged by desire, confusion, and fear, all vague and yet persistent.

John Keats felt similarly. (He was dead at twenty-six, so his was hardly idle fretting.) In his sonnet "When I Have Fears," he speaks about his dread of dying before he's had time to form the poems he knows are in his mind. He is still twenty-two in February 1818 when he writes,

When I have fears that I may cease to be
Before my pen has glean'd my teeming brain,
Before high piled books, in charact'ry,
Hold like rich garners the full-ripen'd grain . . .

KEATS CAN BEHOLD but not possess. His mind is alive with images, memories, thoughts, and feelings, but how can he transform them into verse? He is filled with unpenned thoughts and, perhaps, a sense that he lacks adequate facility for his purposes; he knows what he wants to do, but not how he'll do it. He is apprehensive. Keats's biographer Walter Jackson Bate aptly but too blandly observes about the sonnet, "Every strong desire breeds the fear that it may fail of accomplishment, if not in one way then in another."[1] What Bate has no cause to mention is how such fear can sometimes drive our effort forward and other times transform it into clouds of self-doubt and arrest it.

Inhibiting fears may come to us directly, but often they impede us by appearing in guises that distract us from their essence; they mask themselves. You don't quickly think, "Oh, I'm terrified of failure." You think, "I'd rather go for a walk than sit inside writing on a sunny day," or "I don't know what made me think I wanted to do this. How silly," or, more directly, "I doubt I can do it."

Plenty of people lose interest in their work because satisfaction doesn't match effort. But some turn away defeated because they have paid too much attention to their fears. Others hesitate to begin because the doubt and angst they experience on the threshold keep them from setting forth. Often, when I talk with patients, friends, or colleagues about why they haven't, in spite of repeated expressed desire, started sculpting or weaving or working at a practice they wish to learn, they'll say simply, "I am too busy." And that response is true as far as it goes; many people are too busy surviving to concentrate on mastering something else.

Indeed, when I observed aloud to Alistair MacLeod, the author of pitch-perfect short stories about coal miners and fishermen in Nova Scotia, that the best fiction has often been written by the first generation that moves away from the communal life and stands slightly outside of it—still having lived it, knowing all its stories, but now separated and observing it—he answered succinctly: "There has first to be a chair. And time for someone to sit in it." Sometimes, every waking hour is taken up—whether in mending nets, kneading biscuits, and splitting wood to feed the stove, or in our time-consuming contemporary labors.

However, the effort of pushing worries and fears—such as the fear of failing—out of our conscious minds and hiding them from ourselves can also keep us overoccupied and too mentally busy to focus on the work. As I suggested, the mental energy that we use to keep our anxieties out of our awareness is energy that could be freed up and used on behalf of our creativity. When we let ourselves know and name our real apprehensions, their power tends to diminish, and we can focus more on our work. What if, for example, you are that first generation with time to sit in a chair? Among the unconscious or semiconscious worries you carry may be fear of wasting the opportunity that the sacrifice of previous generations has created for you by educating you. You might fear being disloyal by besting your uneducated parents. Or, because the unconscious holds contradictory feelings, you might simultaneously fear your own wish to best. If what you are doing is alien to your family, you might fear their ridicule and disapproval—making a fool of yourself in their eyes. Or, if your mode of creating requires reflection and introspection, you might fear encountering your psychic pain as well as the collective family pain from the past. You might fear your own inadequacy. You might fear the depth of your desire to succeed. You might fear the fierceness of your competitive instincts. You might fear harming people you love. You might fear the particular strain of hard mental work. You might fear the long periods of practicing, sometimes with little immediate gain. And you might fear failure.

Finding the latch is not simply about choosing something to work at; it's about agreeing to enter into a complicated psychological space filled with ricocheting emotions. Nor is entering enough; you have to learn to tolerate the feelings within it while you find your way with a piece of work. A big reason people give up mastering art-making or complex crafts is that they believe the disheartening sensations they encounter are uniquely theirs. In reality, while such feelings may cleverly costume themselves to intimidate each of us, they are intrinsic to the undertaking. They are the attendant distress of a creative practice.

Daily pleasure is present in craft and creative work, but happiness of the sort James described is more about the satisfaction that comes from living in the complexity of an effort and less about continual feel-good sensations. I am not suggesting that you're going to feel awful all the time, or even a lot. Who would sign on to such a venture? But if you try to do something that really matters to you, you will tangle with some significant bad feelings along the way. Rather than happiness as contentment, an absorbing errand leads you toward happiness as the fulfillment that comes from doing something difficult and personally meaningful.

Think for a moment about *The Pilgrim's Progress*, a bestselling allegorical novel of the seventeenth century and another good way to picture the psychological effort I describe. The hero, a pilgrim named Christian, sets out to reach the heavenly city and encounters many troubles en route. Even before John Bunyan told the story, most people intuited the arc of the tale. Or they knew it from religious parables or earlier narratives, wherein heroes encounter obstacles and seductive temptations they have to resist in order to prevail. (If *The Pilgrim's Progress* feels too fusty, think of *The Lord of the Rings* or other contemporary allegorical tales. All can be understood—on one level—as narratives of mental states the hero experiences while encountering obstacles in the pursuit of a desired end.)

Christian traverses places like the "Slough of Despondency" and the "Doubting Castle owned by the giant Despair." On his journey, he meets a virtuous companion, appropriately named Faithful. When Christian and Faithful attempt to make their way through the treacherous territory of Vanity Fair, they are arrested without cause. Despite his obvious innocence, Faithful is tried and found guilty by a jury of unsavory sorts not so subtly named Mr. No Good, Mr. Malice, Mr. Love Lust, and Mr. Live Loose. He is then scourged, stoned, pricked with swords, and finally, almost mercifully, burned at the stake. Bunyan's account is more than a tad over the top, fervent in its appeal for religious faith, masochistic to the eyes of a modern secular reader, and yet peculiarly suited to our purposes because *The Pilgrim's Progress* vividly illustrates how difficult a mental journey can be and thus why a person might hesitate on the threshold.

The story also reminds us how allegory can usefully picture common feeling states that occur in the course of a larger mission. The abstract is embodied so that we can recognize the enemy— Mr. No Good's name says it all. Allegory may be old news, yet it makes visible the invisible and offers solidarity. Alone in our desks or studios working at our practices, we encounter uncomfortable feelings with no means of identifying them. We do not quickly comprehend that these very anxieties are intrinsic to our own progress. We experience them as being about our personalities or our singular failings, and consequently, too often, they debilitate us and arrest our forward motion. Furthermore, because contemporary culture is obsessed with superficial notions of happiness, it sets us up to feel ashamed of feeling bad. Mental distress gets too quickly interpreted as pathology or weakness. This skewed understanding makes it harder to stay with the challenging psychological journey of mastery. You might—as I still sometimes do because they can seem so convincing—forget that the unpleasant mental states the effort imposes are a normal part of your progress. They are not a sign that anything is wrong with you.

Like many, I often begin a project with a light heart. The first days or weeks of writing feel warm, sunny, and excited. But sooner or later inclemency descends; the horizon darkens. A fine cold drizzle trickles down my neck and coats the lenses of my glasses, so it's harder for me to make out the features of the territory. My mood worsens. I lose my way, turn up my collar, and hunker down. I feel baffled by the psychological turbulence that is awakened in me. Something threatening rustles in the underbrush. A coyote? A feral dog? I am alone and uneasy. My breathing mimics the animal's own shallow pant. I want to run. I have met up with a predicament, but a true measure of its threat is obscured by the gloom. Is it fanged and hungry, readying to spring? Or is it some snuffling herbivore waddling home from a watering hole? Because I cannot distinguish its nature, self-doubt assails me. It whispers to me that I am a fool, opines that the whole outing is misguided. *What makes me presume . . . ?* I start to picture the blurry faces of all my more able peers and forbearers. I ponder my frailties.

And then I come to. I remember that this creepy feeling is recurrent, this lost place familiar. I may not have been exactly here before. Yet I have many times felt a similar chill seeping into me. I remind myself that relief will come sooner or later if I return to my desk and keep writing.

I partly learned to recognize the alien territory thanks to a couple of sentences in a book by a colleague I read around the time I was writing my first book. Contemplating the experience of a patient who was beginning to work as an artist, the psychiatrist Leston Havens wrote, "She learned, for example, that one must welcome discouragement and anxiety in any creative task because they may be signs that will and control are giving way to something fresh and original. She had grown up among people who were convinced that anxiety was a sickness and not the freight of worry, even despair, that any difficult work carries with it."[2]

"*The freight of worry, even despair.*" I copied this paragraph onto a file card and placed it on my desk. Welcoming discouragement may be too much for most of us, but reconsidering it seemed plausible. Havens's description helped me grasp the unlikely relationship between bad feeling and fresh thought; furthermore, he reassured me that distress is a normal by-product when the mind churns. And he implied that it can be a marker of progress. Not only is the content of the paragraph well chosen, but also there's something about the phrasing that makes it particularly ripe for borrowing. It clarified my thought: "She learned this thing that ran counter to her intuition and emotional experience. Maybe I can learn it, too."

II

JOHN KEATS FELT caught between his fear of failure and his fear of death—primordial, wrenching fears, both. One big reason the fear of not succeeding assails us fiercely is exactly, paradoxically, because a certain amount of failure is another inevitable part of our errand. It is built into the whole creative effort, an inherent vice, a flaw in the circuit tripped in the process of delivering the mind's contents into the actual world. Not only is each of us hobbled in our own way, but also it is a rare day when anyone can realize a work as fully as she or he has conceived it. The very desire that motivates us to express ourselves also leads us—and others—to contemplate the distance between what we intend to produce and the actual object. As Richard Wilbur put it,

The soul descends once more in bitter love
To accept the waking body . . .[3]

THE DREAD OF dying without having first produced "books in charact'ry" is the obvious, useful, and perhaps only effective counterweight to the fear of failing. In his own meditation on death, the novelist Julian Barnes quotes Shostakovich as opining, "Fear of death may be the most intense emotion of all. I sometimes think that there is no deeper feeling."[4] And while in part the assertion strikes us as a "duh," we treat it as such to ward off its truth and our own terror. But its subtext is "carpe diem"—seize the day.

It is popular now for people to transform fear of death into "bucket lists"—of the things they want to do, the places they want to see, before they die. Keats's bucket list, if you will, included (second only to his sexual and romantic hungers) the urgent need to write as many poems as he could. And if you feel a similar desire, that there is something you must create before you die or some commitment to art-making you must make to gain adequate meaning in your life, then you likely possess the necessary stuff to step forward across the threshold. Talent and effort will define how quickly you gain mastery and how much you ultimately excel. But deep, itchy, miserable, private longing can stir the glum prospect of *not* beginning and offer you a shove.

We mostly learn to bear our fears by gradually getting to know them. In time, they surprise us less, and so we become more selective about swallowing whole their warnings, or we can be quicker to free ourselves from their grip. But starting out, we sometimes need an assist. And while the support of other people is always important, it helps—in the diverse ways I'm illustrating—to bank one fear against the other.

To counterweight fear, make a wager against it. Put something at risk—your pride, your finances, your free hours, your self-image, or your ideal of who you want to be—something you dislike losing. One successful writer allowed herself to go into substantial debt as she labored over her early work. She bit her nails down to the knuckles, but she also used her peril to sharpen her effort. I don't recommend anything that dramatic for most of us. But there's something to be gained by imitating her gamble in smaller ways. Essentially, you create a fear of not beginning that rivals your fear of setting forth. Announce to all your friends that in a year you will have learned to blow glass well enough to make each of them a vase. Or get your bandmates to agree that by next summer you will have written twelve songs and recorded an album. Or promise your younger sister that by the time she weds, you will be able to build her a bed. If you don't care (or dare) to go public to others, go public to yourself. Make a deal with yourself that within three years you will have tried to publish a short story in twenty online or print journals.

I know my own example is a little quirky, but I learned a lot about how to bear the fear of trying something I didn't believe I could do by walking twelve hundred miles one summer across a chunk of the United States with David—then my boyfriend, now my husband. It was 1976, the year of the nation's bicentennial, and we decided to mark the occasion by exploring America on foot. We told friends and family of our intent, and although many warned us that we were stupid and reckless (two people offered us guns), talking it up with everyone in earshot increased our obligation to deliver.

And I did feel terrified. Not so much of weird strangers or violent neighborhoods, but of my own weakness. I'd never been athletic. I didn't know if I could walk ten miles, much less 120 times that distance. Still, I sensed that learning what my body could do would strengthen me for other challenges—like the long apprenticeship of becoming a psychotherapist, and like learning to write. And once we had talked up our intention, my pride was on the line. I didn't want to have to live with myself as someone who couldn't do what I'd claimed I would do. One terror was matched by another.

Within hours of our setting out in eastern Pennsylvania, reality set in. My too-tender feet blistered in my boots, my shoulders and back ached from the pack; I felt dizzy recognizing the real labor before us. Lacking any sense how to endure my fear, I spontaneously invented a mantra: "The only way out is through." Somehow, repeating it as I limped along—together with David's company—soothed me just enough to let me keep going until, after several weeks, my body toughened adequately to carry my weight. Three months later, euphoric, confident, and fit, twenty-five miles in a day seemed like nothing, and we might have flapped our arms and flown the final miles to our friends' farm in northern Wisconsin.

I learned concretely that although the fear I felt watching a dry streambed suddenly flood during a storm might usefully inform me where not to pitch a tent, I was also often wise to ignore its threats. The developmental psychologist Robert Kegan once described fear as a dog that barks at any stranger, incapable of telling friend from foe. It awaits our guidance. I began to learn that lesson while walking.[5]

THE TENSION BETWEEN the two perils of failure and death, and his effort both to bear that tension and name it, creates Keats's lines. I earlier referred to the pressures that allow art to come forward. One must stay still yet actively seek. One must allow opposite fears to scrummage and shove against each other. A work of art—in this case, Keats's sonnet—is a solution to a problem, an answer to a question even if we sometimes don't initially know exactly what we've asked. And our response—our creation—only emerges if we can tolerate the conflict awakened by the warring pressures. Or, to put it another way, by bearing initially irreconcilable opposites, we force the unconscious mind to seek a compromise. The mind wants to get out from under the torque. The more we can stand our own uncertainty and discomfort, the more attempts our brain will make to mitigate the situation.

The material that emerges is then guided by, or perhaps even coalesces around, the artist's or artisan's technique, which dictates the shape of the solution. Keats wrote a sonnet—a classic poetic form—fourteen lines, *abab*, *cdcd*, *efef*, *gg*. He channeled his emotion and images so they flowed into that particular template. To go from the verbal to the tactile, from poetry to food, think for a moment of a pastry bag filled with a chocolate crème. When the pastry chef twists and squeezes the bag hard, she pushes a decorative fluting out through a small, incised nozzle. The process is pressure, resistance, shaping. The unconscious mind often progresses similarly. Whether the conflict is the large existential matter of failure versus death that meets you immediately as you step out, or smaller, more specific technical problems that define each step of a particular creative production, you have to bear the tension between opposites until your mind has time to create a resolution. And the more you stay with the tension, the more opportunity you have to arrive at something fresh. Rilke's description of how Cézanne solved the problem of the color gray illustrates the point well. Cézanne refused the notion of gray as gray. By resisting any quick decision, by staying unresolved, he gradually forced his mind to perceive the other colors that comingle within what we perceive as gray. And by doing so, he created paintings with unrivaled depth of color.

> *For gray, literally gray, cannot be found in Cézanne's pictures. To his immensely painterly eye it didn't hold up as a color: he went to the core of it and found that it was violet or blue or reddish or green. He particularly likes to recognize violet (a color which never has been opened up so exhaustively and so variously) where we only expect and would be contented with gray; but he doesn't relent and pulls out all the violet hues that had been tucked inside, as it were; the way certain evenings, autumn evenings especially, will come right up to the graying facades and address them as if they were violet, and receive every possible shade for an answer, from a light floating lilac to the heavy violet of Finnish granite.[6]*

I DON'T KNOW what it felt like for Cézanne to paint his way so deeply into the predicament of gray. And, in truth, I can imagine few things I would like more than to inhabit his mind for a day and perceive the world through his sensibility while still holding the separate awareness of myself perceiving him. But since Cézanne's mind is no more, I will simply observe that for me, with my more average mental processes, the energy involved to make my way through an everyday writing problem is pulsing. I attend hard, then I turn away and wait, and then attend again. I can sense a kind of churning within myself. The trick is tolerating first the effort and then the delay as the mind labors. A particular sentence may take seconds, minutes, hours, or days, and I have to bear both the blank periods and the dross that bubbles up in the meanwhile and the accompanying frustration, angst, and doubt. Then I have to assess if the emergent "solution" satisfies me or not. If not, I re-pose the question to myself and start again.

People write about "aha" moments when the work, or a sizeable piece, arrives as a whole. Occasionally that happens, but more often the necessary pieces emerge slowly, and I play with them the way I might finger unfamiliar objects of metal or wood to try to understand their place and purpose. Most I discard. Some I keep for a while and then move somewhere else—or toss. Others fit where I put them. I can spend a day puzzling out what I want to say in a paragraph only to look at it a week or a year later and realize it's muddled or useless; and out it goes.

Often I find that during the hours after I have worked— walking, or dawdling in traffic, or spacing out in the shower, or chopping carrots—other bits of answers float up. Unfocused time is useful, even critical to forward movement, but only after the mind's gears have been engaged and are cranking on the problem.

Obviously, not all creative moments are resistant and difficult. And some people possess a native facility. The poet Gary Miranda, addressing Walt Whitman in a poem, describes Whitman's overflowing mind: "that world you owned like a lamp you could not stop rubbing."[1]

The line has stayed with me for years because it captures Whitman's unstoppable cascade of images and the erotic energy that fuels creative impulse. Stories abound about musical notes, paintings, and words that trip out of people's minds too fast for their hands to scribble. My impression is that moments of great fluidity arise for many reasons—one of which is the native gift or genius; another, the amount of time and effort you have previously invested in the practice. Intense emotional circumstances can also be fertilizing, though usually not immediately. But the relative ease of such efforts suggests that in some cases the unconscious mind may have already somehow worked through or resolved the particular dilemma(s) before any tool is in hand. A famous example (and there are many) of such apparent ease is George Frideric Handel writing the music for the *Messiah* in twenty-four days. John Singer Sargent is said to have rapidly sketched and painted his masterpiece *El Jaleo* directly onto the canvas, rarely reworking detail or looking back. E. B. White recalled having written *Charlotte's Web* so quickly that when he finished it, he put the manuscript in a box for several months "to let the body heat out of it." Not until it cooled a little could he examine it well and see what he'd actually written.[8] (Similarly, I remember hearing in a college class that the photographer Harry Callahan used to put rolls of negatives he'd shot into a shoe box for two years before printing them, so time could grant him a more objective eye for his own work.)

In general, the space in which a person pursues creative mastery is a many-sided one, supported and timbered by the demand that we endure emotional tension in order to solve those problems that occur as we set out to capture something ineffable and make it tangible so that it can become at once pleasing—or meaningful—and ineffable again in the viewer's mind (i.e., the emotion and memory of a Cézanne portrait or Rilke's words). And even to begin the labor we must find a way to endure the warnings fired by our normal psychological defenses that tell us to shut off these unsettling mental processes. Rather than obeying, solving a problem requires that we resist the "bar the door" messages and thus deny our self-protective reflexes. We have to talk down our own defenses and let ourselves feel vulnerable.

We have defense mechanisms, Freud suggested, and his daughter Anna later elaborated, in order to keep disturbing feelings from taking over our minds, impeding or altering our daily lives, or interfering with our sense of our own virtue. Sometimes these feelings are unconscious sexual and aggressive impulses (as when patients come to me blushing and spooked by alien behaviors they enjoy in dreams). Sometimes they are intense or traumatic memories. Other times they are responses stirred up in relationships (as when someone approaches us with more intimacy, or hostility, than we're prepared to meet, and we mentally step back). Our defenses work to keep us functioning as steadily as possible. And they are willing to sacrifice whatever they have to—be it emotion or shared reality—to maintain psychic balance as best they can. But creative production particularly requires that we surface the very feelings, images, and mental states we would normally attempt to keep at bay.

If, riding to work on the bus, you glimpse a person you were in love with years ago, and intense feelings of melancholia, desire, embarrassment, rage, tenderness, or guilt well up inside you, your defense mechanisms work to help you tamp them down so you can mostly settle yourself in time for your 9 AM meeting. Perhaps you will dream of the relationship that night or confide in a friend, but for the rest of the workday your defenses attempt to suppress the turbulence. However, if you want to translate the feelings into the written word, or into a painting of a lover glimpsed through a window, or into a string quartet on the theme of fractured love, you cannot afford to have them settle completely. You must encourage the feelings to linger or return to mind as you attempt to capture, mold, organize, and transform them into your work of art. (Sometimes it is more accurate to say that you must tolerate them when they flood in—occasionally with such intensity that they temporarily knock your feet out from under you.)

Marcel Proust relates a moment in his own childhood that illustrates how disrupting our defenses can be deeply unsettling. Early on in *Swann's Way*, he recalls himself, as a young child, watching figures projected from a magic lantern move along his bedroom wall. "I found plenty of charm in these bright projections," he muses. "But I cannot express the discomfort I felt at such an intrusion of mystery and beauty into a room which I had succeeded in filling with my own personality until I thought no more of the room than of myself. The anaesthetic effect of custom being destroyed, I would begin to think and feel very melancholy things."[9] Throughout *Remembrance of Things Past*, Proust ponders the role of habit. Here he hints at the way creative desire upends the everyday, disrupts our routines for making life manageable. (Little wonder we hesitate.) It does this, he suggests, by overlaying the more exotic, alien qualities of the imagination upon the familiar mental space—a space kept quasi-novocained by routine and, he implies, dulled by the normal functioning of our defenses. When he notes "I would begin to think and feel very melancholy things," he is exactly describing the psychological experience of defenses relaxed in the service of creative effort. The intrusions agitate us. We feel restless, disturbed, at once awaiting the arrival of a further sensation, a feeling, a memory, or an image or thought we cannot fully anticipate or control and simultaneously preparing to try to trap it and rearrange it to our purposes. The contradiction, current countering tide, makes us groan in our moorings.

When we agree to isolate and amplify the brain's productions in the service of craftsmanship or art-making, we are agreeing to becoming unsettled. Yet Proust is equally aware that artists need order to manage the psychic chaos stirred up by creative effort. Habit is the ballast that allows the uncargoed schooner to stay upright as it captures the wind. Habit is what helps us stay put when fear of death and fear of failure clash like cannon-heavy frigates. It's a delicate balance. And it might shed light on why both psychoanalysts and working artists find that daily work, or at least a predictable schedule, structure, and frequent appointments—with a therapist or with one's work space—seem to facilitate the unconscious flow.

I find that the longer I am away from my writing desk, the more the project hardens in my absence. Like cooled iron, it must be reheated before it can be bent further. Nascent writers who come to me asking how to begin seem unhappy or perplexed if I pass along the commonly offered advice that they devote regular, predictable time to sitting at their desks—like three two-hour blocks each week. Carving out time is daunting, but I think people also hope that art or craft will unfurl from inspiration, and that if you simply ready yourself internally, it will arrive. Occasionally perhaps, but I more often receive a communication from within if I am at my desk, keyboard at hand. My father used to love to tell the joke about the poor man who prayed week after week and with increasing anger to God to let him win the lottery. Finally, God, beleaguered, bellowed down to him, "If you want to win the lottery, you first have to buy a ticket." The ticket, my father believed, was his own disciplined effort and labor, his years of preliminary practice, his endless willingness to revise and rewrite.

III

READING ON IN Keats's sonnet, we learn that the poet is filled with longing and with an intense wish to realize romantic passion.

> *When I behold, upon the night's starr'd face,*
> *Huge cloudy symbols of a high romance,*
> *And feel that I may never live to trace*
> *Their shadows, with the magic hand of chance;*
> *And when I feel fair creature of an hour!*
> *That I shall never look upon thee more,*
> *Never have relish in the faery power*
> *Of unreflecting love!—then on the shore*
> *Of the wide world I stand alone, and think*
> *Till Love and Fame to nothingness do sink.*

KEATS ANTICIPATES TWO unbearable losses: dying before he can bring forth the volumes within him and, worse, before he can consummate love. Keats's father, mother, and one brother had all died by the time he turned fifteen. A second brother, Tom, died soon after he concluded this sonnet—with the poet as bereft nurse at his bedside. Keats hoped his own constitution would prove heartier, yet I would be surprised if he ever felt certain of the next cup of tea, much less of an open-ended future. What the future could bring was for him a luxurious speculation beside the immediate one of whether he will have any future at all. His tenuousness, his profound uncertainty really, propels his pen. The sonnet also hints at the way sexual love and self-expression comingle and feed off each other in complex ways, something I return to later. For now I want to underscore Keats's terror—the aspirant's fear writ large, shared broadly in less dire forms by all who have stood daunted before a creative wish—that one will die without having found opportunity to transform fancy (words, images, musical notes in the mind) into something tangible like short stories, stacks of paintings, musical scores, and so on. (Simply identifying with his sentiments may be a good measure of our own need to make art or craft. If we are strung with even slightly similar strings, his sense of urgency is powerful enough to make them vibrate sympathetically.)

When Keats wrote these lines, he felt well, though the tuberculosis was already burrowing into his lungs. Within two years, his health had vanished. The sad unfolding that followed is well-known to devotees (and now to viewers of Jane Campion's film *Bright Star*). On a cold, raw day in early February 1820, to save money, John Keats traveled home from London in a seat on top of the stagecoach. He had forgotten his "warm great coat." By the time he reached Hampstead, he was chilled through, feverish, and very ill. He stumbled into his bedroom, barely making it onto his bed before his lungs hemorrhaged. His housemate and friend Charles Brown famously described the night:

> *On entering the cold sheets, before his head was on the pillow, he slightly coughed and I heard him say,—"That is blood from my mouth." I went towards him; he was examining a single drop of blood upon the sheet. "Bring me the candle, Brown; and let me see this blood." After regarding it steadfastly, he looked up in my face, with a calmness of countenance that I can never forget, and said,—"I know the colour of that blood;—it is arterial blood;—I cannot be deceived in that colour;—that drop of blood is my death-warrant;—I must die."*[10]

KEATS KNEW JUST enough medicine—from brief study, from nursing his dying mother and brother—to recognize that the bright red blood was newly oxygenated, arterial, and thus the harbinger of certain death from tuberculosis. I first read Bate's biography forty years ago, and I have recalled this moment since. The account is haunting, like icy hands around one's neck, not simply for what it reveals about Keats's life, the fate it names, but as a metaphor for the most helpless sort of self-knowledge: You cannot argue with the fact visible upon the sheet. You cannot finesse the news it delivers to you about you. It is incontrovertible.

One overarching job assigned to our defense mechanisms is to allow us to maintain an adequate denial of death, and of our own limitations, to get about our lives. To see so clearly and yet continue on is remarkable, however much Keats may have felt no alternative. In return for his courage, he benefited from having his knowledge catalyze his creativity. Now or never. The moment also captures another of the great tensions that can freeze us upon the threshold. I have proposed that the first is the fear of dying without having expressed ourselves versus the fear of failing. When we open up that fear, nearby or nestled within it we can see two other threshold fears. One, as Havens and Proust illustrate, is the fear of disrupting our habits and enduring new, difficult feelings versus the fear of retreating into deadening custom, or never setting forth. A second, suggested by Keats examining his own blood, is terror at the prospect of looking with clear eyes upon ourselves and our experiences as art-making requires, not cowering or turning away, but somehow bearing what we see.

CHAPTER 3

---

recognition

I

ONE OF THE more arresting photo shows I've seen, called *Lives I've Never Lived*, was a small exhibit in the late '70s by Abe Frajndlich that consisted of portraits he'd taken of the photographer Minor White, who died in 1976. In the photographs, Frajndlich shows White dressed up in different costumes representing other lives he might have lived. What, the exhibition asked on White's behalf, would it have been like to have had more than one turn? Who else might I have become? What other work could I have done?

When these pictures were taken, White had already survived three heart attacks and was about to meet up with a fourth that would prove fatal. Like Keats, he saw the scythe. His artistic response, of dressing up—donning costumes and personae—and posing for portraits, offers a motif for exploring another among the psychological tensions that impel and impede art-making. It allows us to ponder what it means to costume and reveal ourselves, and particularly it lets us explore the hide-and-seek people play around the phenomenon of recognition.

By "recognition" I do not mean fame, but something much more basic: the fact of feeling *seen* or *not seen* by others and judged by them as "us" or "not us," worthy or unworthy, estimable or contemptible, lovable or unlovable. Andy Warhol's bon mot that everyone gets fifteen minutes of fame—and thus, implicitly, that everyone hungers to be famous—collapses a more complicated series of psychic realities and wishes into its most narcissistic aspect. People hunger for basic, loving recognition, and the American fantasy of fame is this recognition on steroids. (In truth, many Americans now feel so anonymous that as a nation we suffer from what I might, tongue in cheek, call "recognition deficit disease"—a disorder that overfeeds the hunger for fame.) But that word "recognition" fuses two different wishes and functions, one crowd-focused, the other more intimate.

The question, If you see me fully, will you find me acceptable? is one of the core questions of life and of art-making, and while we often try to keep the worry mostly outside of consciousness, it is powerful. When we feel strongly fearful, however unconsciously, that the answer is negative, it sometimes impedes creativity and creative mastery. At the same time, creative play—like the pictures of White—that gathers its energy from that fear, and works at appeasing or outwitting it, can be one of art's rich sources.

As the title of the exhibition (and later the book) declares, each of Frajndlich's photographs describes something forsaken—a life White did not choose. Although now, on death's brink, he cannot turn back or begin again, he *can* imagine himself living these alternatives. The hourglass has pretty much emptied, yet fantasy flows. In one portrait White appears as a car mechanic, in another as a priest. In a third he sports a dark leather jacket, jeans, and a T-shirt with "Ball Buster" written across the chest; he defends himself or perhaps slightly menaces us with a thick chain he's wound around one hand. A fourth photograph finds him lying on a daybed in his underwear, a top hat covering his crotch. A fifth shows him sandaled, wrapped in a blanket, presenting himself as a Greek philosopher. A sixth, taken only weeks before he died, entitled *Dance with Death*, reveals an emaciated, bare-chested man clad in black tights, his thinned skin draping his ribs. The sun is strong, angled; dark shadow alternates with bright highlights. The dancer's hair is long and white. He stands before us, arms posed in mock formality. His legs are crossed, almost but not quite in a classical ballerina's stance. Although Frajndlich declined White's invitation to photograph him without clothes, in *Dance with Death* the costumed man seems laid bare.[1]

White died before they could finish the project. And Frajndlich includes an eerie portrait of the photographer in a coffin. In the context of so many disguises, the viewer wonders if the corpse is really dead or only practicing—dressing up. Has White donned another costume? Are the two men playing? This time they are not.

Cameras, costumes, and creative fantasy push against boundaries and limits; they toy with time and death and identity. Imagine yourself putting on outfits that allow you to assume other personae or to express previously quiescent aspects of your personality. For White and Frajndlich, the game of "dress-up" provides artist and subject with free space in which to explore, even as mortality crushes in. It is a way of anticipating death, and it is child's play; clock time moves forward into the future, and the images simultaneously attempt to re-create what would have happened in the past, had such a past ever existed.

The clothes together with the camera "solve" the mortal only-one-turn problem by offering magical replication (a gift dependent on the camera's essential asset of allowing us to preserve and reprint images) so that a man suddenly possesses multiple lives. The immortality is provided by art's prerogative to calve possibilities.

II

I RECALL THE *Lives I've Never Lived* exhibition as having been by equal measures intriguing, funny, sad, brave, and poignant. Poking around online, I found and ordered a copy of the out-of-print catalog. When I examined it, it mostly confirmed my memory, though the White I reencountered in Frajndlich's introduction seemed more difficult and elusive, contradicting the whimsical personality I'd assigned him thirty years ago. I also found online several treatises on White's closeted homosexuality. One life he'd apparently not lived until he was quite close to death was that of a man free to express his sexuality openly. I remember when I first looked at the photographs, I sensed their sequestered eroticism and experienced them as a kind of ambiguous "coming out," though the fact was nowhere ascertained.

The photos toy with mortality even as they signal the fates readying to snip White's thread, and they grieve. At the same time, they allude to secrets and in-jokes that mystify the uninitiated viewer and seem to comment on the hide-and-seek nature of gay life thirty-five years ago. The two men are partly raising the question of how to present White's sexual identity, and how much of it to hide or show. In this sense, costuming offers a sexual treatise, and it also comments on actual social danger. Meanwhile, the art-making allows the forbidden or conflicted aspects of himself (of ourselves) to exit down the fire escape—to find egress without too blatantly calling dangerous attention to themselves. Among the queries that seem to accompany the pictures are ones like, Can I reveal myself to you? If so, how? What form must it take to hold your attention in a fashion we can both bear? Or must I stay alone with my experience? What do I need to keep secret to survive?

Art-making of all kinds (not simply the confessional strand, nor simply about the self) often creates a whirlpool from questions of revelation. What is too much? What is too little? What will alienate the audience? What will captivate them? How should I costume my effort to make it succeed? Frequently, the answers become the technique: a series of choices about how one presents intimate feeling or material—the art of art. Often people's initial discomfort overwhelms and stops them—the surprise of seeing blatantly what you know, or accidently exceeding what you thought you chose to show, or spilling a secret, even if it's invisible to others. Meanwhile, the trick, to the degree there is one, is to recognize your upset as yours, not the public's, and as inevitable, and often temporary. In a sense, you're looking at the work with public eyes while it is still in process, and not ready for such a viewing. That kind of imaginative examination can usefully inform you about ways to alter it, but if it overwhelms and prevents forward motion, it is interfering. Resolving the bad feeling means returning to the material and exploring different ways of "costuming" it so that it hides and reveals according to your psychological and aesthetic needs.

Meanwhile, the very notion of a costume captures a contradiction that ideally energizes creativity: Because I am "disguised," I can reveal myself more. Because of the doubt I create—What is me, what is not me?—I can show more to you while still guarding my privacy. The novel is "fiction." The self-portrait is "only a painting." The song is tossed off. The photograph is me "wearing a costume." Artistic privacy in certain art forms (and thus, to a point, artistic freedom) rests on maintaining ambiguity about the artist's relationship to the material revealed. In 1862, in a moment of unusual frankness, Charles Dickens confessed to his admirer Fyodor Dostoyevsky, as Dostoyevsky later recounted in a letter, that "there were two people in him . . . one who feels as he ought to feel and one who feels the opposite." From the one who felt the opposite, Dickens claimed to have "made his evil characters." From the other, he noted, "I try to live my life." He attempted to channel into his fiction the parts of himself he despised, "his cruelty, his attacks of causeless enmity towards those who were helpless and looked to him for comfort, his shrinking from those whom he ought to love." The raw emotions and mental states tormented intimates yet, when funneled into vivid characters and thus successfully costumed, offered energy to all he wrote.[2]

III

IT IS THIS costume motif as it relates to recognition that leads us closer to one of the most essential among the complex psychological tensions involved in mastery and art-making. White's dress-up is both playful and serious; it comments on variation, liberation, identity, danger, sexuality, and mortality; there can be many interpretations. But the most interesting to me is the commentary the photographs provide about the tensions around recognition and, with it, survival, love, and loss of love in art-making. If we allow Shostakovich's claim to stand that the most intense emotion is fear of death (and one would be hard-pressed to argue), the second is the fear of confirming that we are not acceptable, not a member of the family or the tribe. In a sense, the second is a corollary to the first, because for many—certainly the young and the helpless—to be rejected is to be abandoned and left to expire exposed on the mountainside, like Oedipus for example. Even when the outcast survives, he is often lamed by the experience.

Indeed, the story of Oedipus demonstrates well the importance of recognition in art. Once again, when we typically think of the word "recognition," we think of its public dimension as in "White is recognized as a major twentieth-century photographer"; "We recognize *Oedipus Rex* as one of the greatest plays ever written." And while it always carries bits of that public meaning, I want to use "recognition" here in a more psychological, certainly a more intimate, sense—the decision of "us" or "not us." And Sophocles's *Oedipus Rex* offers a remarkable illustration of recognition so defined.

Right after Oedipus is born, his parents, King Laius and Queen Jocasta, are warned by an oracle from Delphi that their infant will grow up to murder his father and marry his mother. Desperate to outwit fate, his parents command a shepherd to expose the baby on a mountainside. The shepherd disobeys and rescues the infant, who survives and is adopted and raised as the son of King Polybus of Corinth. Oedipus grows up ignorant of his real parentage. Consequently, when he strikes and kills an insolent man with whom he disputes right-of-way on a road, he is unaware that the man he murders is his father.

When Sophocles's *Oedipus Rex* begins, Oedipus has been made King of Thebes following the unsolved, mysterious murder of its previous king, Laius. He has married the king's widow, Jocasta. A pestilence has befallen the city. The streets are littered with corpses. The country is in crisis. The gods declare that the plague will only end when Laius's murderer has been brought to justice. Oedipus turns to the blind seer Tiresias to find Laius's murderer, and Tiresias accuses him. Although Oedipus and Jocasta at first deny the possibility, its truth gradually, inexorably, emerges. Oedipus has in fact murdered his father and married his mother; Jocasta has married her son. Unable to bear the horror and dishonor, Jocasta hangs herself, and Oedipus gouges out his own eyes.

The commonly told story of Oedipus that focuses on the tragic hero as an adult clips the full psychological arc of the tale. For our purpose of illustrating the dilemma of recognition, emphasis is better placed on how the deadly cycle is set in motion by fear: particularly by the parents' fear of a prophecy about their own mortality. Told by the Delphic oracle that their infant will grow up to murder his father and marry his mother, they abandon him. While the concrete meaning is plain, the psychological meaning is richer. Laius and Jocasta are king and queen, but neither power nor wealth makes them immune to death.

It seems that the king and queen cannot bear the emotional contradiction of being at once so powerful and yet so vulnerably mortal. They rule their known world, but the laws of nature condemn them to share the common human lot of aging and death. Even though they are royalty, if they "recognize" their infant as their son, they tacitly agree to submit to feeling the helpless love devoted parents feel for children, and they tacitly agree to watch his maturation become their death knell. It is inevitable. The Oedipus tragedy is set in motion psychologically because the parents' love for their infant cannot swell within them adequately to overcome this terror of the emotional and generational pain implicit in new birth (i.e., the passing of their own virility and top-dog status).

Their infant portends their replacement and death and thus represents an unbearable challenge to their sense of omnipotent power. (The fate of each parent symbolizes a different aspect of the fallacy of resisting time, of reaching for immortality. The father who does not give himself over, who rejects his child as a way of trying to stop time from killing him, is punished by being murdered by his son. The mother is punished by not aging appropriately to her years and thus remaining as the ready, incestuous bride for the next generation. Had she accepted time's demands, she would be a grandmother now, not the older wife of a young man.) The parents fail to recognize the newborn as their beloved son and to allow that love bond to trump their fear and vanity. Meanwhile, their urgency to know the future, to query the oracle, is itself a wish that undermines love, since love generally demands that we fly blindly and take what comes.

Rescued and adopted, Oedipus lives. But he has been damaged and rendered emotionally blind by his parents' action. He does not know where he has come from or who he is. He is unable to recognize himself, so, in turn, as an adult, he is unable to recognize Laius or Jocasta as parents with whom he must honor the taboos against patricide and incest. When, at the end of the play, Oedipus blinds himself using his wife/mother's broach pin, the ghastly act concludes the drama's motif of emotional blindness with a literal enactment.

Rereading *Oedipus Rex* 2,400 years after it was written, we shudder much as Sophocles's own audience must have. The play sits on a lode of psychological knowledge. I am using it here as a parable of the urgency human beings feel about being recognized by loving, appreciative eyes. Few desires are as primal. Think of the sentence "I recognize you." Hearing it, we feel two strong, opposite meanings. On the one hand, it offers instantaneous relief. *I am not alone; I am not anonymous; I am safe. I am among my own; I am valued.* But just about as quickly it summons something chilling—perhaps out of Grimm—as when we have hidden from some dangerous, gigantic person and have been found out. Then it conveys an array of threats: *You are powerless; you are alone; you are prey; this may be the end for you.*

We know that an infant's survival rests on parents' or caretakers' basic capacity to recognize him as their own and thus worthy of nurture and protection from predators. It's not hard to see why juvenile humans would be motivated, even hardwired, to enhance their winsomeness, nor why they would possess many unconscious and conscious strategies for doing so, nor why these strategies would become braided together with the motif of recognition. While we tend to think more about self-enhancement (lipstick and stiletto heels, good pecs and a full head of hair) as reproductive strategies to promote the survival of one's egg or seed, it seems far more likely that pubescent efforts to be sexually "recognized" rest on the earlier effort of survival. If you do not recognize me as your desired infant, I am unlikely to live long enough to reproduce.

Everyday physical costuming—a haircut, a tattoo, eyeliner—is one of the ur-creative impulses. I will seek to define myself, to declare my affiliations, to effect or even to control how you see me. Art similarly enhances self-display: A flower garden, or anything beautiful we create, is a kind of peacock's tail. While it is by no means art's primary task, it does convey the message *There is more to me or to being human than what shows on the surface, exactly because I can alter that presentation at will.*

Part of the essential energy behind creativity is the way artists enact their quandary about basic "live or die" recognition. The creative process functions de facto as a kind of costuming, rather like the way someone might dab perfume on a rabbit's nose to encourage her to adopt and nurse an orphan bunny whose status as "other" would otherwise be revealed by its smell. The artist is always dabbing perfume, always confusing the terms of recognition. At the same time, the artist's creativity is made more potent because it has this life-and-death substratum.

Perhaps the eeriest, certainly the most popular, contemporary commentary on the recognition dilemma is the video of Michael Jackson's song "Thriller." Filmed in 1983, viewed by tens of millions of people worldwide, and declared, in its day, the most successful music video ever made, the fourteen-minute film uses classic horror-film motifs to explore the ambiguities of recognition and the questions I described: *What's me, what's not me?* and *If you see me fully, will you find me acceptable?*

You need to know almost nothing about Michael Jackson's overdocumented life to grasp that while he wasn't exposed on a mountainside, he was so badly abused by his parents, particularly his father, Joe Jackson, throughout his childhood that he might just as well have been set out on the rocks to perish. The abuse took diverse forms: One was physical beatings when he made mistakes dancing or singing; a second was denigration of his body and physical features; a third was putting him in situations where, still a child, he witnessed all manner of sexual acts; a fourth was Joe forcing his own grandiose goals onto his children and driving them to precociously master musical and performance intricacies—no matter what the emotional cost; a fifth was the parent using terror to promote his children's psychological submission.

Like Laius, Michael's father was apparently unable to recognize his children as they were and could only appreciate them according to how well they served his own wishes for wealth and fame. While this parental stance is hardly uncommon, the elder Jackson took it to an extreme.

A word commonly used by bloggers is that Joe turned Michael into a "machine"—an apt cliché that captures just how intensely dehumanizing the process was, the way it destroyed playfulness and pleasure and poisoned Michael. Even a casual reading of his life leads you to conclude that the drug overdose that killed the King of Pop (like Oedipus and Laius, Michael, too, was a king) in 2011 at the age of fifty was the predictable end of an insane and profoundly tormented existence.

Listen to the song "Thriller," and you hear a description of the terror of a child waiting to be abused—what I referred to as "being recognized as prey"—the opposite of loving recognition. "You try to scream, but terror takes the sound before you make it / You start to freeze as horror looks you right between the eyes / You're paralyzed" or "You hear the door slam and realize there's nowhere left to run / You feel the cold hand and wonder if you'll ever see the sun."[3]

The *Thriller* video complicates matters. In front of the camera, Jackson becomes the feared abuser—someone who is alternately loving and terrifying. Like Oedipus, Jackson cannot know himself, but for a different reason from the tragic hero. He's been so pummeled and coerced (a kind of mind-smashing "whack-a-mole") that no well-defined identity can emerge. In lieu of a sense of self, he remains possessed by his tormenting progenitor, and his psychological options are to submit or evade.

In the video, Michael's victimized role in childhood is taken by a nameless, sweet girl he is courting. One Michael, the likeable half of his video alter ego's split personality, treats this girl with tenderness and consideration. Michael transforms into a killer right after she agrees to "be his girl." Her yes shuttles them both instantly into the chaotic, murderous world that mirrors his experience of familial intimacy. He begins to make an ambiguous confession to her—"I'm not like other guys. I mean I'm different"—but his story is interrupted by his physical transformation. What was he about to describe? Pedophilia, plastic surgery, suicidal intentions, rage, profound identity confusion? We don't know, because becoming a "werecat" at once deprives him of language and/or rescues him from having to openly state some intimate truth.

Whereas Frajndlich's photographs of White show one person in various sets of clothes, Jackson pushes costuming many powers of ten further—into the life-and-death realm of witness protection. Not only did he wear the sequins and white glove, the bobby socks, turned-up jeans, the uniforms of all sorts, the endless costumes for his music videos, he also had his face surgically rearranged and then compulsively sliced again and again until it became grotesque. Perhaps, from our perspective, he is using surgeries to become either the son Joe might recognize with love or a stranger Joe wouldn't recognize as "his." While White is playing, Jackson is fleeing for his life—yes, ambitious; yes, fabulously rich; and so successful that he eventually inhabits heights where oxygen deprivation carries you beyond loopy into brain damage. He is, it seems, deeply desperate, a man-boy trying to keep a step ahead of self-knowledge, self-loathing, and his sense of being pursued by a deadly stalker.

And yet, amazingly really, during his multiyear flight, Michael Jackson created the most universally successful songs and videos in the history of media and music. His popularity speaks not just to his talent and seductiveness, but also to the way his extreme search for a bearable "self" caused everyone's lesser but similar desire and conflict to resonate. On the one hand, people who had only experienced normal—universal—struggles with these questions of lovability could find solace in his themes, and on the other, fellow sufferers could use him and his songs for inspiration. As one blogger named "Dave" poignantly observed in an online discussion entitled "How exactly was Michael Jackson abused by his father and why?", "I am far more a coward than MJ, he turned his life into something great and all I can do is hide in my room all my life with these scars unable to do anything out of fear. R.I.P. Michael, if there could be any inspiration for my life it would be you."[4]

Jackson was an amazing performer and a weird, brilliant creative force. Among his more interesting music videos are the two versions—directed by Spike Lee—of *They Don't Care About Us.*

In them, Lee and Jackson transform Jackson's own experience of not having been loved into an anthem for all the world's downtrodden—and, to a lesser degree, everyone else who has ever felt undervalued, hurt, or even just a little overlooked. The first version, shot on the streets of Rio de Janeiro, is strange and vivid; the second "prison" version is haunting.

The salient point is that for a long time Jackson managed to keep going. Though he was fleeing madly, his talent and ambition kept constructing chutes and ladders to support his flight. Ironically, his father's goading had forced him to an extraordinary level of skill, even as it, and the family life and child-star adulation that accompanied it, implanted a group of deadly sleeper cells that gradually destroyed him. His life-and-death emotional conflicts were so bald and intense, so plaintive, that the music that sprang from them was experienced by many as true and irresistible. Meanwhile, his extraordinary fame brought ever more public scrutiny of his psychological torment and improprieties. At first, he used his huge riches to build a sanctuary. But, gradually, his masks and costumes no longer created enough ambiguity to shield him. His needs leaked forth, no matter how hard he tried to cement them in, and they were more radioactive than any costume could cover or gifted artistry transform. After being charged twice with sexually abusing young boys, how could he not have felt that he was either too fully seen—or else grossly miss-seen—and, either way, globally declared too damaging even for *his* artistry to redeem?

IV

As FRAJNDLICH'S PHOTOS and Jackson's videos both illustrate, costumes riff on this anxiety of recognition. And they temporarily free the self from the burden of its particularity by creating a fantasy play space. When you flip through the pages of portraits of Minor White, you feel amused and intrigued but also a little unsettled to see the same face emerging from such diverse garb. When you watch *Thriller*, the unsettled feeling trumps. The costumes in which we dress, and the emotional sensation they create, are at once us and not us. This "between" place—where the mind's productions materialize into the physical world—is not only where we often live emotionally, whether overtly costumed or not, but also is another way to describe both a realm where we broker loss and a space of creativity.

THE PSYCHOANALYST D. W. Winnicott named this between space "transitional"—a place where the imagination partially overcomes helplessness and loss by investing inanimate objects with emotional energy and thus animating them and creating a realm of illusory experience. (Think costumes and recognition.) Winnicott's famous example is of an infant relating to his stuffed animal. The infant endows the foam, cloth, and button eyes with his own feeling life. But because the toy is an actual object outside of himself, the act is a compromise. The object can be used to represent the role the infant assigns it. Yet the object and the baby are not one. Winnicott writes, "I am here staking a claim for an intermediate state between a baby's inability and growing ability to recognize and accept reality. I am therefore studying the substance of *illusion*, that which is allowed to the infant, and which in adult life is inherent in art and religion."[5]

Art-making begins in the moment the baby has a feeling first about the teddy bear and then for the teddy bear. Creativity, Winnicott brilliantly speculated, first tests its muscle in these earliest actions of the youngster's effort to make his fantasy life reach toward an object in the world. (His observations work for me better in relationship to toddlers and young children than infants, since babies offer up very little about their imaginative life.) By making such a connection, the toddler attempts to bridge the distance between subjective need and objective possibility, to use fantasy to create an illusion that allows him to experience a bearable accommodation with the world around him.

In this sense, the earliest creativity is in the service of emotional survival. The stuffed animal may become a playmate, or an alter ego, or a partial proxy for a parent or caretaker, one that can be mostly controlled, that stays nearby, engaged and attending, when the actual person is absent. The transitional object, like a bundling blanket for the psyche, allows the young child's emotional life to continue to retain heat in the absence of the adult. If the absence is not too prolonged, the psyche does not have to shut down to survive. The toddler remains connected with the world in a link modulated by his capacity to cocreate an illusion.

By imagining himself into the costumes, by allowing them to reflect aspects of his psyche and his desire, White enters the transitional space and brings the clothing to life. Using the camera, the two photographers create an illusion of multiple lives; they explore how White has lived but one life among many that were possible, an idea that gains poignancy and power as it both nods to and resists White's impending death.

Desire for or, sometimes, conflict about reattachment in the face of emotional loss energizes the transitional space. The toddler may long for the missing parents yet feel anger, even hate, toward them for leaving. But the toddler also seeks to explain the other's absence. And since survival is so deeply based in attachment, the question instantly becomes one of how to maintain it: how to present oneself as worthy of "recognition." The hide-and-seek commences as, simultaneously, do efforts to embellish the self.

Perhaps artists are people for whom the question of being recognized contains more urgency. Perhaps artists are like Oedipus, unsure of how firmly love's grip holds them; perhaps on some level they are always hoping not to be left exposed on the hillside. Or perhaps they simply feel acutely aware of these basic human predicaments and wish to represent them. Perhaps *Oedipus Rex* takes its dramatic power from the psychological concerns the playwright loaned to his hero, and the act of writing was Sophocles's own psychological hide-and-seek.

Through costuming the artist also reveals, or reminds us of, his fuller self-portrait: his pragmatic dimensions, his scamp impulse, his plasticity, the way he seeks to slip out of his own shoes and into someone else's, to trick, to merge, to escape, to invade, to possess more than his apparent due. The person in the process of creating lives the contradiction *To be myself, I do not have to be myself.* He seeks recognition for the work almost as a deflection from the self. He manipulates his materials and consequently manipulates the terms of recognition. *How much am I the person you think you see before you, how much the denizen of an invisible, timeless space, the mistress of a private, ineffable process that yields the hand-crafted table, the stained-glass window, the glazed pot?* Iago in *Othello* speaks for Shakespeare, for artists everywhere, and for the whole craft of playwriting, when he declares, "I am not what I am." In fact, Shakespeare's Protean capacity, the way he so brilliantly fills out so many voices, the way everyone speculates about "who Shakespeare really was," is as good a cultural representation as exists of that elusive plasticity.

How often have we heard someone say that they made an effort to meet a performer or artist they admired and felt disappointed? The pianist was aloof, the actor inarticulate, the sculptor embarrassed, the writer petty and uninterested in us. Their dismay testifies to how hard it is to accept that the self-expression that gets elaborated in art does not necessarily flood into the rest of the being. In her essay "Talking about Writing" Ursula LeGuin humorously observed, "Anyway, meeting writers is always so disappointing. I got over wanting to meet live writers quite a long time ago. There is this terrific book that has changed your life, and then you meet the author, and he has shifty eyes and funny shoes and he won't talk about anything except the injustice of the United States income tax structure toward people with fluctuating income, or how to breed Black Angus cows, or something."[6]

Conversely, people not infrequently tell me that they have a memoir or novel they long to write. In part, they are passing along information. But what else are they confiding? Often they describe a hunger to revisit experience and to reconstruct it, to express it and have it recognized. This wish, too, has kinship with costuming. It is as if they have a pearl-embroidered gown stuffed away in the closet. They possess a richer, more elaborately detailed narrative of their own lives than any they can put forth into an everyday venue, and they long to communicate it, to have it known, and perhaps, in turn, to be seen as its owner, protagonist, or creator. "My day job is not all I am" is a pervasive, life-saving identity statement.

Much of Henry James's previously mentioned novel *Roderick Hudson* turns on the question of whether Hudson, a sculptor, possesses unusual genius—worth "investing" in—or whether he is a semicharlatan who can chisel a great statue or two but who will burn out. Roderick's first fine pieces draw much interest to him, and he's soon the favored guest at fancy Roman dinner tables. Is he in costume as a great artist, or is he the genuine article? While, on some level, the question is disingenuous and naïve, it makes reference to an interesting negotiation of social power.

Being "recognized" as a fine artist offers Hudson a passport into elite social circles. He gets taken up by benefactors who want their own status confirmed by association with him.

Through Hudson, James poses an artist's query—perhaps his own: *How am I seen? How do I measure up, where do I belong in the scheme of things? How can I costume myself to gain some control in this game? Am I Oedipus, an abandoned infant or a king? Am I a beggar? Or am I, if not Oedipus, perhaps Odysseus disguised or costumed as a beggar, scorned by those better clothed who encounter me on the road, but really a lord returning home to string my bow, take back my hall, and reclaim my wife from the feckless suitors?*

People who wish to create often recognize within themselves the sense of agitation and unease—as Keats describes in his sonnet—of Odysseus disguised, of holding something within that has not yet emerged, of having hidden power. With that awareness comes a tension. It is as if you are carrying a large valuable item invisible to others—something that cannot be recognized because it cannot be seen. Similarly, early on, people who want to create often ruminate about the credibility of what they're sensing. They ask themselves the question the Roman gossips ask about Hudson. *What is real, what is costume? How does one tell?*

Well, in fact, one essential telltale of the genuine is precisely your willingness to endure the anxiety of living in the dilemma of recognition, bearing it, bearing its longing and disappointments, giving yourself to the work without being able to know the outcome of the intimate, vulnerable effort. In our Progress, the pilgrim's peril vis-à-vis recognition comes from the temptation to try to forsake sacrificing time and effort, to forsake the risk of laboring, to eschew brokering the real dread of coming up short—the dread of being recognized but not embraced. And there's no way to achieve the skill, content, and polish needed for success without taking on this challenge and then coming up short countless times. The wish for recognition is fundamental to our psychological being, and our urgency to survive, and our longing for love. The process of mastery requires tolerating the wish as it falls short and falls short, until finally it may approach something plausible.

V

RECOGNITION AND COSTUME figure greatly and relevantly in the denouement of Homer's *Odyssey*. I will remind you that when Odysseus finally returns to his home on Ithaca, Athena disguises him as a beggar so that he can gather news and assess how endangered he is and how to proceed to repossess his wife, Penelope, and his kingdom before the rude suitors become aware of him and perhaps attempt to kill him.

Toward the end of story, when, after a decade of battle and a second decade of wandering, Odysseus finally arrives back at his palace, the person who first recognizes him, as Erich Auerbach so memorably discusses in *Mimesis*, is his old nurse, Euryclea. (This scene, though it predates *Oedipus* by several hundred years, uses Euryclea to answer the later play on the matter of love and recognition. The nurse is not highborn, yet she is willing to bear the price of love, so she recognizes him.) Bathing the feet of the supposed beggar, she glimpses the scar on his thigh and cries out. Neither time nor costume can negate her memory of her charge's body and his childhood hunting injury. (His scar might be understood as the sum of his particular growing up. She conveys to him that his past has been witnessed—known, and remembered with tenderness.) While the wish each person feels for recognition may have a complex, private genesis, this story confirms that the desire more universally derives from our earliest experiences of care and love. Only someone who loves us intimately might know the secret markings on our bodies—the scars, birthmarks, and other idiosyncrasies that are ours alone. Euryclea's devotion is archetypal. In the scene she transcends her servant status. Her apparently mundane powers, giving care and love, become elevated and almost godlike. She sees through time and costume; she recognizes us; or, more precisely, she recognizes us scars and all.

A core tension that overarches art-making is between being invisible or even obscured, or endangered (as by the suitors), and being recognized with loving eyes. Part of the wish for recognition that artists feel can be captured by the Odysseus story. It is a wish to recover the psychic cum mythological place where the hero or heroine has just returned from a difficult separation and is being bathed anew by something like pure love, a place where time has stopped and where death is held at bay. Part of the risk of art-making is the fear that you will take on the psychic wish, make yourself supremely vulnerable, and fail.

Think back now to Keats's urgency expressed in his sonnet "When I Have Fears." A portion of the confusion that exists for him—the way writing the unwritten poems and feeling recognized by his beloved seem so tangled together—springs from his many losses, and the sense that art functions to restore love by costuming the artist in a way that will not only attract contemporary attention but also simultaneously restore the original, lost, devoted eyes. Although the proposition is impossible, the tension of the desire and its inevitable disappointment energize creativity. Paradise is lost; art-making is search and rescue.

CHAPTER 4

shame

I

T HE FAILURE TO find loving recognition can produce a difficult, desolate mental state in and of itself, but often the void is made worse because, in the absence of acceptance, like brackish water pools in the ruts of a dirt road, it fills with shame. Shame includes many unpleasant and perplexing sensations, but we can most simply understand it as an intense, unbearable feeling that our core self has been glimpsed and revealed as undesirable, a feeling of awful self-consciousness that makes us urgently wish we could disappear.

Shame is so potent a force that it can stop aspiring artists in their tracks. It sometimes comes into full view, but even its slight, distant sneer is intimidating. Without thinking, we may inhibit creativity and mastery so as not to summon its attention to ourselves. If I were wagering which feeling most often impedes art-making, shame would be one good bet. But, as with the other obstacles we've described, shame is not simply a threat, but also one of the great turbines of mastery. People's efforts to become accomplished are often impelled by their urgency to evade or metamorphose their sense of shame. The poet Robinson Jeffers wondered, "What but fear winged the birds?" And, similarly, many works of art are winged by the artist's wish to transform shame.

Learning to traverse the emotion helps you survive art's long apprenticeship, and it offers perspective on a significant psychological underpinning of the artistic process. If we return to our allegorical primer, the illustration of Shame would show a big brute in our path. She wears seven-league boots. Dodge her at one crossroad, and she waits at the next. Yet, depending on whim or God knows what, she will either clobber us or lift us onto her shoulders and spirit us forth.

Some years ago, I heard a chilling instance of the public shaming of an aspiring writer. A well-known, serious, and accomplished novelist and essayist was a guest on a Boston radio call-in program speaking about her work. A caller identified herself as a fan and a writer. The novelist asked her what she'd written. Not too much. Had she published? No. Well, the novelist icily opined for all of radiodom to hear, You may write but you are not a writer.

It was night; I was alone driving somewhere, but I gasped aloud. The caller sounded terminally mortified. She stuttered a bit, simpered, and hung up the phone. My own impression of the exchange was confirmed when a patient who'd also heard it spontaneously brought it up in her session—as evidence that she, the patient, ought to feel ashamed that she even wished to write. The power of the single comment was remarkable. The elder writer, with one sentence, managed to throw many listeners into a state of shame.

I understand the elder writer's irritation. She had devoted her life to her work. If you claim to be a doctor without attending medical school, you will be sued. Pilot an aircraft without a license, and officers with guns will arrest you. If you want to call yourself a writer, according to this view, you must first earn your stripes through effort, dedication, sacrifice, and visible accomplishment.

Still, one traditional draw of the arts has been that a person can learn them outside of school—either with apprenticeships and the help of mentors or through solo study and trial and error, usually with both. But no exams, or licenses, or required degrees yet bar the way for aspirants. This open gate is critical. Art-making is an essential part of life, and the more paths artists have to mastery and to gaining authority in their work, the better, even as no particular path offers a guarantee.

Thomas Mann once observed that writers are people for whom writing is harder than it is for everyone else. Serious artists often work at their craft for many years before they begin to go public. The demands are rigorous. But since the effort is private and not widely visible, the arts also invite dilettante fantasies: I'll just pick up a pencil, and in no time *voilà*. To someone who had worked a lifetime to obtain her position, the caller must have resembled a bedbug waiting to be pinched.

All the same, my own sympathies were equally with the younger writer. The scathing put-down foreclosed a conversation. I wished someone had asked her what was getting in her way. What was keeping her from putting more words on paper, or joining a writing group, taking a workshop or class, talking to a psychotherapist, or somehow figuring out the architecture of the missing bridge that, once in place, might allow her to better pursue her desire? And what mix of foolhardiness, desperation, and bravado caused her to approach a tigress and set herself up to be swatted publicly? Being a therapist, I could not help but wonder if she were enacting the very fear of being shamed that hobbled her in the first place.

Or could she have tripped over the residual gender shame some people still feel as they approach art-making? What had she observed when young about roles men and women were supposed to play? Did she grow up with some contemporary equivalent to "Women can't paint, women can't write," as Charles Tansley so famously proclaims in *To the Lighthouse*? Until very recently, female artists who crossed over—out of sewing, singing, dancing—into "male" areas tended to be dismissed as ridiculous and shameful for trying to do something that was beyond them.

In *The Mikado*, Gilbert and Sullivan spear "that singular anomaly the lady novelist" as one ripe example of a contemptible species. Perhaps the older writer's ferocity was partly the legacy of her own struggle with such prejudice. (Male artists, in their turn, may be charged with inadequate manliness. "What were they like as schoolboys?" the poet X. J. Kennedy muses about poets. His humorous answer captures the poet's bumbling, macho-less image. He is someone who is "always chosen last," "the kind that squirmed at hurt cats," who "shrank from touching cracked-up birds," who had "to ask to have their fishhooks wormed.")[1]

Serendipitously, I read two memoirs in close proximity, Julia Child's account of her life in France and how she learned to be a first-rate cook, and Renée Fleming's story of becoming a world-famous opera diva. While there were many differences between the women and the skills they set out to master, I was struck in both books by how extraordinarily hard each one worked in private for years and years before going public, certainly before becoming famous, and how each managed shame. Both women loved what they did and thus brought to bear a similar, and I suspect key, willingness to stay with their efforts through eons of study, practice, and improvement. Both had the ability to hear criticism and to make corrections repeatedly without becoming terminally discouraged; to bear the anxiety of their efforts; neither was too proud to learn and keep learning. This willingness to be taught and corrected, without feeling ashamed, sometimes over and over again, is a huge asset when you are seeking to do something very well. And one way shame impedes people is by making them take criticism too personally—as about them rather than about what they're trying to learn.

In Fleming's case, mastery meant—to pick one example among many she offers—working rigorously to improve her voice range, gradually finding her high notes, and then attending carefully to everything from mouth shape to diaphragm strength, to mental imaging, to vocal cord flexing, to shoulder tension—so she could count on hitting the notes cleanly and gracefully almost all the time. For Child, mastery included studying at Le Cordon Bleu school in Paris, practicing endlessly while alone in her own kitchen (if you saw the movie *Julie & Julia*, you will remember Meryl Streep chopping all those onions), gathering mentors, teaching cooking, and finally working daily for most of a decade to test, alter, and test again the recipes that went into her first volume of *Mastering the Art of French Cooking* (a best-selling volume that many publishers passed on before Knopf finally bought it). Each woman was willing to attend to every tiny detail of her craft in order to get better at what she was doing.

Both women experienced strong emotions and strong reactions about all different aspects of their lives, both encountered plenty of obstacles and hard times, yet neither one let herself be stopped by shame. Renée Fleming tells of getting ferociously booed while performing a Donizetti opera in La Scala, the great opera house in Milan. It was her first time on that stage, considered one of the pinnacles in any singer's career, and some purists in the audience really disliked her vocal flourishes. While it's clear from her account that she felt mortified and deeply unsettled by the ruckus, she was able to find ways to shake off the shame (commiserating with other singers to whom it had also happened helped a lot) and—amazingly—to perform on the same stage again only six months later.[2]

So, too, every viewer of Julia Child knows that the television episodes are filled with potentially mortifying moments, as when she drops some *pièce de résistance* on the floor, picks it up, and resettles it upon the serving platter, reassuring her audience that no guest need be privy to what goes on in the kitchen. A chunk of her star appeal is exactly this seemingly unembarrassed attitude toward herself and her own mistakes. The common knowledge both women grasped is that public gaffs are inevitable; they are part of the work, not revelations of secret, fatal flaws. Your task, if you want to succeed, or even just to continue performing, is to work through the unwanted feeling of exposure and keep going.

In contemporary America, simply committing yourself to art-making brings you perilously close to shame's precipice because—whatever your fantasies of stardom or best-sellerdom—in fact, the effort to master something difficult and complex usually involves a sacrifice of income. By unscrewing a tube of oil paint, you are taking exception to the national creed that the business of America is business. Especially if you're a committed amateur—mastering an art form, craft, or discipline primarily for the love of it without much public ambition—there's little doubt you're ratcheting down the income conveyor belt. You're using time in contradiction to Ben Franklin's famous admonition that it "is money." What did you do this morning? I sat at my pottery wheel and stuck my thumbs into balls of clay and threw away the unsatisfactory results. Then I stared into space. Always, there's a voice somewhere whispering, *You are being self-indulgent; you could have spent the time working at something lucrative.* The violin-maker Sam Zygmuntowicz observes, "Our society has gotten more materialistic . . . People go into professions to make money. There's nothing like the traditional craft that you do in your village, where you go into it when you're twelve and seven years later your apprenticeship is done and for five years after that you're a journeyman and by the time you're thirty you can open your own shop."[3]

The pressure of bills is very real, and it can be horrendous, sometimes life-destroying. Possessing enough money to dissipate chronic worry does make life better. However, there's a distinction to be made between the safety provided by having adequate money to know you can pay the rent or mortgage without putting off other bills, and the cultural brainwashing that insists that the only status of worth comes from having ever more financial success. (Noting this excess, Freud was said to have referred to America as "dollaria"!) Were our culture more nuanced in what it values, were it willing—as it has been for occasional nanoseconds in the past—to offer genuine respect to diverse endeavors, people would feel greater permission to focus more on serious pursuits that provide other satisfactions.

I still own a pair of sandals handmade in the 1960s (one such nanosecond) by a leather craftsman in Vermont. They were so well cut and sewn, I was able to wear them for forty years before retiring them. Being seen in shoes that do not keep pace with fashion is itself deemed slightly shameful because our "throw it out" culture casts a judgmental eye. But I, for one, would be thrilled if we nudged ourselves back toward valuing what is well conceived—and built to last—over what is designed to quickly become landfill.

II

To better understand shame's place in art-making, it helps to know something about its larger psychological role. I sometimes think of shame as a group survival reflex in which the individual is an afterthought. Shame's first goal is to have you conform to group expectations. To deliver its message, the gods hold you by one toe and dip you into its oily vat. You don't think shame; you feel covered in its viscose grime. The great hand immerses you whenever you are told you are, or believe yourself to be, violating a basic communal code: if you're observed behaving in a fashion deemed unseemly; if you're caught practicing some sexual or gender behavior that others around you frown upon; if you're a member of a denigrated group perceived as not abject enough; or if you're accused of overpromoting yourself, taking more than your share from the dinner pot, speaking up when not invited, shirking a duty, soiling yourself.

Shame is a survival mechanism. It guides you to behave well enough not to be cast out of your group, useful since in the past survival depended more frankly on group interdependency. (In part, shame is an extremely powerful, life-and-death emotion that lingers on millennia after it was most needed.) Shame works as the enforcer of a family's or group's particular codes. Shame on you for . . . removing your clothes in public . . . running from battle . . . seducing your brother's girlfriend . . . embezzling your mother's retirement fund . . . calling yourself an artist . . . or sometimes simply having the gall to exist at all. If shame doesn't arrest a particular behavior, it inclines people to hide it. And holding a secret deemed shameful erodes a person's confidence that he or she can be loved. *If you knew who I really was, you would not love me* is a common thought, and often shame-inspired.

Shame, the trauma psychiatrist Judith Herman has succinctly observed, "is a state of unbearable self-consciousness." At its most intense, it can make you writhe. When you are overcome by an acute shame attack, you feel overheated, revealed, scorned. You imagine that you are an object of jest—or worse. You want to flee; you want to shield yourself from the many soul-invading eyes that expose you—whether in reality or in imagination.[4]

It is a person's desire for acceptance—his fundamental wish, described earlier, to recognize love in the eyes of "the other"—that makes him subject to shame. What if, when you look for affirmation, you find disgust instead? While the occasional wave of bad embarrassment is perfectly manageable, intense or chronic shame has an insidious, corrosive effect. When suffered repeatedly or over time, shame tends to demoralize people so deeply that it dulls their whole sense of self. What's worse, people feel ashamed of feeling shame! So those who live with a lot of it may hunker down and decide that the less said, and the less attempted, the better.

The difficulty in naming shame is part of what gives it power to impede art-making. Often, the fear of feeling shamed stops people from staying with their effort, but they don't process it directly as *I'm anxious about showing myself and what I can and cannot do; about making art I think is good and others think is bad, and thus being painfully exposed and derided about something that really matters to me.* Instead, many folks experience their shame worries indirectly—as profound yet nebulous discouragement, hopelessness, and general malaise. *What's the point?*

Shame heats up when you are perceived to be attempting, even silently desiring, to rise above your assigned caste or station—when it appears you think more of yourself than others think of you. (The feeling may have evolved in part to stabilize social hierarchies of dominance and submission: who is Alpha, and who is Omega.) Think in how many novels and movies the servant girl or poor kid gets ridiculed for possessing aspirations that her circle deems an overreach. "Look who's putting on airs." The intention of the comment is to discourage her fantasy or her wish to possess more than those around her deem her due. The derision can be just plain mean, or it can be protective—as from a parent who can't bear to anticipate the way the world could harm her unchecked child. People who seek to create often fear receiving—and sometimes do receive—a variant of this kind of remark: "Look who believes he can act!" or "She thinks she can paint, bless her heart."

The disconnect between our somewhat atavistic hardwiring and the demands of the current world—particularly the demands of individual self-expression in art-making—ties aspiring artists in knots, since most live outside the constancy of a single group and its more coherent expectations. We refer to many contexts at once—work, family, neighborhood, various friendship networks, new places we visit, and all that we carry from our pasts—and we are often not quite certain what is expected of us in a particular one. Furthermore, shame is transmitted intimately from one generation to the next. A mother ashamed that acting on her intense wish to paint will make her the laughingstock of her circle, no matter what she says aloud, may convey the shame to her daughter before the child is old enough to be aware of what she's internalizing. (And it may linger way after the cultural context in which it was relevant has disappeared.)

The early twentieth-century sex psychologist Havelock Ellis relates this story: "A pupil of Ingres tells that a female model was once quietly posing, completely nude, at the École des Beaux-Arts. Suddenly she screamed, and ran to cover herself with her garments. She had seen the head of a workman on the roof gazing inquisitively at her through a sky-light."[5] What happened? We return to the innuendo of eyes. Apparently, the woman was comfortable in front of the art students because she could imagine herself as their object of beauty, and thus could feel shame-free before them. However, in the eyes of the workman, she saw herself as a woman without clothes seated before a group of clothed men, so she felt naked and mortified.

This slight inflection caused by seeing herself reflected back in one set of eyes as opposed to another reveals how shame can take hold in a flash. It also confirms how dramatically self-love may vary depending on how one defines the reference group—the eyes in which one feels "seen." People today live the art model's tenuousness, but worse. There is genuine freedom in our dislocation, but there is also an uneasy sense that we never quite know the rules (or the eyes) of all the many places we find ourselves. An artist nowadays often imagines his work for one context or audience and finds, to his dismay, that its critical reception represents a separate view embedded within another discourse. One reason status "stamps" such as "I got my MFA from Columbia," or "Knopf published my cookbook," or "When I last performed in La Scala . . ." are so sought, apart from market issues and general competitiveness, is that they serve to make the speaker feel a little more certified, more justified, and thus clothed.

The image of a woman posing naked also reminds us that artists live the predicaments of contemporary individualism writ large. Individual creativity, by definition, dictates that you be visible apart from a group—so, in a sense, each art-maker agrees to embark on the psychological equivalent of posing naked. There can be vain delight in it and erotic pleasure. Yet, the very notion of the person apart immediately alerts shame. "Why is that one over there not blending in with the others?" In turn, shame behaves like a border collie energetically herding errant creatures back from their singular wanderings.

The story of Ingres's model encapsulates the artist's dilemma: In whose eyes are you seen? Are they ones in which you—or what you create—are beautiful? Or are they ones to which you have unintentionally revealed a silly or unpleasant nakedness that displays your deficiencies to no greater end? Have you shamed yourself by openly attempting to produce something original but failing? Where shame is concerned, artists poise themselves on icy slopes. Should they shift their weight onto the wrong foot, they risk a death slide into the abyss, yet, while their balance holds, they stand tall with a grand view.

Performing artists, for example, know that they are exquisitely tuned into their audiences. When they feel their effort falling flat, if the audience is sparse or seems unresponsive, they often leave the theater feeling emotionally empty and slightly embarrassed. They may wonder if they're losing their touch. Conversely, if the crowd is enthusiastic, they take their bow feeling full and stimulated; they glow with well-being. Professionals develop strategies to survive these repeated exposures (and possess different degrees of sensitivity from the get-go), yet the vitality of their work partly rests on their subliminal awareness of the private emotional stakes.

For all its power, shame is not intractable. Nor are accomplishment or applause its only antidotes. Something as simple as loving, loyal, or sympathetic words from another person, especially one whom you trust knows you well, mitigates its force. Humor provides one of the strongest remedies—laughing with friends can dissipate it in a flash. Encouragement drips balm on its abrasions. Recollecting a group in which one feels accepted or esteemed is equally potent.

People also often subdue shame in daydreams in which they fantasize about overcoming their helpless position and embarrassing troubles, ones in which they chase away insult and injury. In turn, such daydreams frequently seed works of art. Privacy is another of the art-maker's best antidotes to detoxify shame. The reason Virginia Woolf's call for a room of one's own has become a rallying cry for artists is not simply because women deserve their share of physical space. Woolf's assertion underscores the larger need for privacy. Privacy grants the artist crucial control over self-exposure. There is the physical privacy—of having a separate work space. And there is the deeper emotional privacy that the physical privacy helps to shelter. Privacy assists the artist in keeping critical eyes at bay long enough to allow the work to gestate and begin to emerge. No one should ever have to display work before she feels ready. There are moments early on in the creative process when all it takes to crush the effort is the slightly raised eyebrow of an observer, especially when his opinion carries weight. Sometimes that observer is internal, sometimes external. I often think of pages written during the early weeks or months of a project as like a soap bubble. Exciting, iridescent, yet so fragile that any wrong poke will end its tentative ascent upon the updraft.

Art-making itself is a profound way people deal with shame. And while this truth may sound trite when said so baldly, it is an essential point. In the most basic sense, creativity is the mind's repeated effort to solve an apparently insoluble problem. Shame is one example of such a problem. One way art transforms shame is by replacing helplessness with agency.

Suffice to say, the impetus for art-making includes a wish to "solve" the great human "obstacles" like helpless pain and inevitable death, not to mention all our diverse, more personal unconscious conflicts. Artists take emotions or events that have happened to them, and that they have sometimes experienced helplessly (with shame prominent among the accompanying feelings in those instances), and then transform them. They move from passive to active. They mold the experiences into narratives or objects or other expressions that in turn allow audiences to grapple with their own perceptions and feelings.

III

SHAME IS A raw material the great comic actor and film director Charlie Chaplin possessed in abundance, and his hilarious and poignant films illustrate how he crafted a remarkable response to the feeling. Indeed, overcoming shame is such a central engine of his work that had his early life contained less of it, while he might have been a happier man, I doubt very much he would have become as peerless a filmmaker.

Chaplin was born in London in 1889. His childhood was miserable. His parents were unsuccessful, poor music hall performers. His father, ill with alcoholism, abandoned the family when Charles was a toddler, and his mother spent time in mental asylums. He and his older half-brother, Sydney, lived from hand to mouth—sometimes with their mother or sometimes in workhouses and worse. It likely helped Chaplin that he discovered early his gift for performing. And either because of or despite his desperate circumstances, he ran with it. (His mother favored him, and her love, however intermittent, may have helped his confidence.)

Whatever the sources of his resilience and luck, the films make clear that the adult filmmaker never forgot the penniless boy's miseries—of wearing ill-fitting clothing, inhabiting bad rooms, erratically attending school, of being periodically abandoned and frequently neglected, unwashed, tormented, and underfed. Chaplin also carried the shame of being known (seen) as the son of drunk or mentally ill parents; of finding himself, simply through his circumstance, to be the object of other people's pity and derision. In his autobiography, to offer one example among many, he describes his destitute mother having no money

to buy him or his brother clothing and so recutting her own garments to fit them, an effort that led to their being laughed at and
teased by schoolmates. Referring to one such garment, Chaplin
recalls, "Sydney wept when he was made to wear it."

In the workhouse the boys were separated from their mother.
Here is Chaplin's recollection of reuniting: "How well I remember the poignant sadness of that first visiting day: the shock of
seeing Mother enter the visiting-room garbed in workhouse
clothes. How forlorn and embarrassed she looked!" In a gripping account, Chaplin goes on to describe being whipped in front
of other boys in the orphanage; some pages later he recounts
being frequently deprived of food and locked out at night by his
father's inebriated mistress during a period when the brothers
stayed with their father.[6]

Early on in the book Chaplin relates what is perhaps the
most revealing story as to how he survived the adversity. As well
as suffering from a mental illness, his mother, Hannah Hill, had
a voice problem that unpredictably interfered with her singing.
One day when Chaplin was five years old, Hannah could not
finish a music hall performance because her voice gave out. She
was booed off the stage. Urged to it by the manager, the little
boy walked onto the stage, took her place, and began to sing a
popular song of the era called "Jack Jones." The young Chaplin
already knew a number of song and dance routines, but he had
never performed in public. After singing the opening verse, he
felt hard objects hitting him. Throwing rotten food at performers

was standard music hall behavior, but he quickly realized that the audience was instead showering him with coins. He stopped to gather them, and his glee sparked theirs. The more he smiled and sang and gathered coins, the more they threw, and his public debut was a rousing success.[1]

To a five-year-old—and in his case one whose family lacked adequate money to provide for him—a shower of coins surely must have seemed beyond magical. And it was *his* voice, and *his* performance, that provoked the tossing. What's more, the moment's emotional power was enhanced because it followed on his seeing his mother humiliated. *He* restored the family honor. The performance demonstrated to Chaplin early on that he was talented in the family business, and his discovery was mightily reinforced by the delight of gathering up many coins. However, what I suspect enhanced its formative power was that the boy learned that he could, through his own actions and talents, transform shame into applause.

A child sees a parent failing and feels ashamed. Likely, he both resonates with the parent's own sense of shame and feels embarrassed for her. She appears maimed and sickly, unable to do what she must do. We imagine him fantasizing about how *he* will save her. She cannot go onstage, so *he* will. He'll sing in her place and make her rich. And he will take care of her in a way his father has not.

What is remarkable about Chaplin's experience is how the reparative fantasy actually was enacted in real life. The gratification must have been intense—and it may well have created a kind of psychic crucible. (In his autobiography, Chaplin points to a catalyzing moment when as a young teenager he was invited to recite a funny story in front of his class. But it's hard to imagine that this later experience didn't already have the bedrock of the earlier one beneath it.) No doubt talent and serendipity coalesced to ripen Chaplin's genius and to allow him to deliver it onto the new medium of film. But it's fair to suggest that his successful first performance—literally a "dream come true"—propelled him psychologically. Furthermore, the story also demonstrates how motivating shame can be: driving him to escape the quicksand of his parents' lives.

For most of us—especially as children—there is a forbidding high wall that stands between dreaming and acting. We daydream so we can wait, so we can enjoy and/or endure our circumstance—which might be one of particular hardship or merely of the universal childhood hardship of, among other things, sometimes feeling small and powerless. For Chaplin, to have success so early must have felt both liberating and terrifying. Terrifying because if he attempted to strut after his triumph, his real immaturity would soon have tripped him up and forced him to see (perhaps with shame) that he was just a little kid. Indeed, the child's mix of bravado and vulnerability later creates the attractiveness of his adult film persona.

The great comic's movies provide a lucid illustration of how the translation process—from shame felt to art created—works, and they suggest how struggles with shame can energize genius. Chaplin's signature character the Little Tramp made his first appearance in 1914, soon after Chaplin started acting in films, in a short called *Mable's Strange Predicament*. A skinny, diminutive fellow with dark, wavy hair, sensitive eyes, and a delicate, almost pretty face punctuated by a mustache, the Little Tramp is a poor man on his own in a hostile world. He strives to look respectable, but he doesn't make the grade. His shoes are too big, his jacket too rumpled, his pants badly hitched. He wears an incongruous bowler hat too small for his head and carries a bamboo cane. Yet he remains an icon a century after he first appeared.

It is no coincidence that in *Mabel's Strange Predicament*, many elements of Chaplin's own youth are apparent. The movie commences with the Tramp out of place in a snooty hotel lobby where his very presence is making rich ladies uncomfortable. Rather than retreat discretely (as shame would dictate), the Little Tramp settles himself comfortably into the plush furniture, pulls out a flask, and drinks himself drunk. His inebriation frees him from "status" shame, and he is able to offend the ladies with impunity. He falls out of his chair, dances about, pulls the tail of one woman's dog, and on and on. He amuses the film audience by behaving shamelessly in a situation where we as viewers know we would feel cowed.

While the great social novelists—Dickens, Zola, Victor Hugo, to name a few—wrote with empathy for workers and the unemployed poor and sometimes from their protagonists' perspectives, and painters like Millet, Toulouse-Lautrec, Robert Henri, and George Bellows painted scenes from back-alley lives, Chaplin's choice to place his character center stage represented a radical departure from these high-art efforts. Rather than portraying the Tramp voyeuristically—as exotic or other, as an object of pity or idealization, an illustration of why life is difficult, or as a poster boy to make a political or moral point, Chaplin's alter ego is an everyman; he's one more anonymous guy trying to make his way in this crazy life. He is irreverent and feisty. He has plenty of mischievous agency, and while he may seek sympathy—especially from a pretty girl—he wants no one's pity.

Though acted upon relentlessly by people with more status and power, the Tramp continually initiates actions, including many that upend manners or break laws. He diddles with the rules of respectability, and he creates a good portion of his own troubles by defying his assigned station. A viewer can rarely determine when he knows exactly what he's doing or when he is simply inept. Within this haze of uncertainty, he wreaks his everyday comic havoc. In *The New Janitor* (1914) he uses his feather duster to dust a woman's behind. In *Police* (1916) with the fruit seller looking on, he brazenly—and hungrily—bites and chews half a dozen of the vendor's fruits and then walks away without paying. (He grabs the laugh by posturing as a dissatisfied, effete connoisseur rather than the starving jailbird he is.) He can be remorseful, sometimes baroquely so, when confronted with his peccadilloes. But his response is pragmatic and polite rather than abject. He is unapologetically himself. And as such he is the first great international mass media "little guy" hero.

Chaplin's comedy is often very much about shame, and arguably, the popularity of his movies rests on the Tramp's ability to meet up with (or invite) and live through one mortifying event after another—without allowing any to impede his progress. Like his early twentieth-century audience—dislocated, often recently immigrated, or moved from rural village to city, short of cash and struggling—he is without power, prestige, or social status, and consequently most circumstances he encounters demean him. But he is marvelously oblivious, and more often than not, his troubles roll off him. The Tramp absorbs a million insults and delivers almost as many. He does not stay down. By the end of a film, he's often bested his enemies and won the girl.

Chaplin manages to create empathy for his wayward alter ego by conveying him to the audience as a person with an inner life they can recognize sympathetically, as someone experiencing moments of sadness and longing during which his wishes—whether to know the rules like an insider or to be less kicked about and more welcomed at the high table—are made visible. Consequently, even the earliest and shortest movies transcend their basic ingredients of chase and slapstick. Chaplin gives viewers the double pleasure of laughing aloud and at the same time subliminally grasping amid the hilarity and jumble that the filmmaker "got" their common plight. At their best moments the films have a sublime poignancy overlaid on their comic essence.

Like singing in a music hall, making a movie for others to watch—taking a creative effort public—is usually a shame gamble. You hope for success and admiration, for an embrace or welcoming reception from the judging "group." You then wait to see if you have achieved the wish. The wager is made edgier because the psychologically high-stakes game is affected at once by some variables you can control like effort, subject choice, and presentation, and others you cannot control, like the biases of judges and the particular enthusiasms of a cultural moment.

The cultural emphasis on individual expression creates the artist's opportunity to explore creative impulses often uncoupled from the more functional ends of craft. And this division is both a boon and a burden. Less is at stake if necessity rules, if the bowls you design are the ones you need for daily use. They must hold soup. And as long as they accomplish that task, any other attribute is value added. The maker can dismiss, the users forgive their aesthetic limitations in the name of their utility. But creative expression that is primarily aesthetic or abstract does not accept the same apology. There's nowhere to hide.

IV

A CLASSIC SHAME scene in *The Gold Rush* (1925) illustrates Chaplin's larger creative use of the emotion. The Chaplin character—a variation on the Little Tramp here called the Lone Prospector—is a down-and-out miner hoping to make his fortune in the Alaskan gold rush. (In what is perhaps the most famous moment in the film, he is so hungry he boils and eats a leather shoe.) The Lone Prospector becomes smitten with Georgia, a saloon girl. He reveals his romantic feelings to her and to the camera. Seeing his underdog desire pulls the audience in. We want him to succeed. Will she meet his eyes? Will she recognize him as someone worthy of her and of reciprocal feeling? Not quickly. Unimpressed by the penniless tramp, Georgia is polite to his face but mocks him behind his back to her female friends, who giggle, whisper, and make fun of him. They imply that his overtures overreach his station. Who does he think he is?

Although the audience gets an eyeful of their disdain, the girls hide it from the Prospector. He extracts a pledge that they will spend New Year's Eve with him—an engagement they have no intention of keeping. We know they dissemble, but he does not. (Perhaps his longing is too intense to allow him to grasp his situation. But it's also a key part of Chaplin's alter egos that they frequently overlook circumstances that would likely mortify their real-world counterparts.) Suspense builds through the next scenes when, spurred by desire, the besotted miner shovels mountains of snow off winter walkways to earn money to pay for the feast he plans to serve. We wait and watch. Will Georgia and her friends show up?

When the camera returns to him on New Year's Eve, the Prospector is in his cabin, and he stands before us cleaned up—in a starched white collar and tie. His hair is very combed. We are impressed by his grooming and simultaneously anxious for him. When the camera then pans across his carefully set table, and we watch him place a neatly wrapped gift at each seat, we find ourselves beginning to writhe. He has made *so* much effort, and his vulnerability is excruciating. We know before he does that he is about to be badly disappointed. As audience we feel the awkwardness of his position, and yet we are relieved not to be in it. Better him than us. We appreciate his enduring our social rejection for us.

But soon we feel grateful to him for another reason. Just when we would like to turn away and free ourselves from sharing in his shame, he spares us by transforming it into something whimsical and risible. As the prospector sits alone at the table and time passes, he gradually understands that Georgia and her friends are not going to appear. His solution? He comforts himself by fantasizing that the saloon girls *have* arrived. The mortified person mentally departs the real moment and, in fantasy, enters "transitional space." There he recasts his experience as he feels it ought to be. He becomes the dashing hero—suave, in control, and best of all, in the company of beautiful women who dote on him and delight in his antics.

In the charming sequence that follows, he is surrounded by the girls who are completely absorbed in him and entranced by him. He entertains his pretty guests by stabbing two forks into two dinner rolls and making the bread "shoes" dance on the table. Well-being is restored. (Something as corny as the dancing shoes falls wildly short as a way to woo women, but because it is *his* fantasy, and his make-believe world, it works splendidly— which adds charm and comedy for the viewers.)

In this tiny moment, the whole larger metamorphosing ca- pacity of the artist's creativity is enacted in miniature. If shame is indeed the whimsical giant as likely to pound you as assist you, Chaplin plays the magic fiddle that makes the brute sweet and ser- vile. Imagination is the antidote to helplessness, the elixir at hand to transform mortification. Part of Chaplin's brilliance is figuring out comic and sad ways to film daydreams. The movies became classics because they do not simply gratify with wish fulfillment the way a cartoonish, one-dimensional effort might. Rather, they insist viewers accept the more complex—and more accurate— pairing that reveals at once the character's actual situation and his fantasy repair. Because of this greater depth—their ability to capture the scope of the psychological conflict—they are able to represent universally shared feelings, and we easily find ourselves within them. Shame provides a fierce energy that urges on the art and creates emotions that bond artist and audience.

Finally, Chaplin's fantasy also offers up another secret in countering shame while you work at mastering a craft or art form. Create a group in which you can give and get support. Surround yourself with a "tribe" of your own—however occa- sionally you assemble. I don't mean just a circle of friends, but a slightly more formal group—that has a task and meets regu- larly—even if it's monthly. Being able to spend time with people with whom you feel a sense of solidarity creates free space. Conversing with allies, and feeling your thoughts heard, shared, countered, and not derided, is a potent way to offset shame. An effective shame-reducing sentence is the commiserative "It's happened to me, too. Ugh."

Even though, as I suggested earlier, it can confuse our shame sensors, the fact that we are not stuck forever in any one geographical location—nor in any one particular world—is also a liberating aspect of contemporary life. It's easy to live in a small village if you are esteemed and beloved. However, if you're unpopular; if you are bullied, harassed, enslaved, or marginalized, your circumscribed existence becomes imprisoning. For all the anomie and fragmentation of current life, it offers opportunities to build "affiliative" groups in which we can spend time with others who share our passions, and whom we enjoy, and who appreciate us.

I have long been in a reading group that has offered me this kind of pleasurable sanctuary. It's not a confessional place, just one where I can exchange ideas, get into friendly disagreements, laugh a lot, and share fond feelings. While, at best, we meet two hours a month, there's substantial carryover. I feel tolerated and more; each time we meet, I am reminded that I enjoy my groupmates, and they enjoy me, and I can take these feelings back with me to my writing table and use them to encourage myself. Good groups take a while to build, and all groups do not succeed. But, if you gradually create one that is positive and lively, then the more you risk—not necessarily in intimate disclosures, but in the willingness to act or speak spontaneously and try out ideas— and the more they can offer back a confirmation you can carry abroad. Yes, you have your share of impossible qualities, but we enjoy and respect you as you are—most of the time. Which is as good as it gets.

I have an artist friend in an artists' group, and I know plenty of writers in writers' groups. Certainly, when they function well, these groups offer more specific support and useful criticism. And if you can start one or join one, they can be invaluable. But groups that are more general in their purpose also work. And there are other ways, like good conversation with a close friend, to recover the sturdy sense of belonging that dissolves shame, but because shame triggers are so group-sensitive, groups often work more powerfully than individual relationships can. A note of caution: The power of a group can work against you, too. And if you start, join, or are in a group where you feel repeatedly denigrated, shamed, bullied, harshly criticized, or ignored, or if one person seems to be taking all the oxygen in the room, try to address the situation frankly, but if it doesn't get much better very soon, leave. Watch a Chaplin film instead and regroup.

CHAPTER 5

creative solitude

I

"I WANDERED LONELY as a cloud / That floats on high o'er vales and hills," William Wordsworth famously proclaims in his "daffodil" poem, a work he composed in 1804 that would become emblematic of the Romantic idealization of solitude in nature, "when all at once I saw a crowd, / A host, of golden daffodils." One feels joy, the poet exclaims, first seeing, then later lying alone and recollecting, the mass of daffodils. "For oft," he concludes several stanzas later, "when on my couch I lie / In vacant or in pensive mood, / They flash upon the inward eye / Which is the bliss of solitude; / And then my heart with pleasure fills, / And dances with the daffodils."

Wordsworth's claim of wandering "lonely as a cloud" and finding joy in nature, and then later experiencing bliss recollecting the scene, embodies a central strand of his poetic thought. What's more, the famous poem helped create our current appreciation for solitude and for individual, autobiographical creative expression. But all is not really as it first seems; Wordsworth's good feelings that day he was wandering were hardly just about daffodils. He was mulling over a whole lot more than flowers. And the emotionally complicated real-life context of the poem tells us much about the actual psychology of creative solitude and the extent to which it often differs from the common, romanticized image of the single artist working in isolation. Many people who aspire to make art stall out in their effort because they cannot tolerate the solitude they arrange. Often their mistake is, ironically, to make it too . . . solitudinous.

Anyone reading Wordsworth's lines would be forgiven for concluding that the wanderer lacked a companion when he discovered the yellow flowers, and forgiven, too, for imagining the speaker as a solitary guy. The speaker, maybe, but not the poet. Or, at least, not in any simple sense. It would seem that Wordsworth himself could not have been less alone when he observed the scene. The daffodil walk occurred during the spring of 1802, a time when William remained enraptured with his sister, Dorothy, and when she continued to feel consumed by her passion for him. Were their mutual feelings not human delight and/or muddle enough, the poet was also arranging to wed his wife-to-be, Mary Hutchinson, one of Dorothy's dearest friends.[1]

William and Dorothy were walking along Glencoyne Bay in Ullswater on the day they discovered the daffodils. He had been off visiting Mary and securing their marriage, which he very much wanted; Dorothy had been staying with friends while awaiting his return; and the brother and sister had happily reunited. As they made their way through the woods to Dove Cottage where they lived, they first spotted a few flowers. Then a few more, and then each step brought into view other clusters growing wild. The unexpected find—so many tossing yellow heads—enchanted them, seemingly with more daffodils than they'd ever seen. The siblings had separated, and when they reconnected there were daffodils everywhere in such superabundance as the imagination could hardly better.

William apparently laminated the memory of finding the flowers together with the eroticism and desire and joy that had infused his day. Although he doesn't say directly, it appears that he did not experience these daffodils simply as an awe-inspiring landscape. Rather, they seem to have been a vivid physical representation of an agitated, exuberant emotional state later recollected and commemorated exactly because of the intense, and perhaps unsettling, passions that accompanied their witness.

When, two years later, Wordsworth wrote the verse (refreshing his memory by consulting the journal Dorothy kept as much for him as for herself) he represented himself (or at least the "I" of the poem) as separated from all female companionship, sustained simply by recalling the blooms. It might have made a cleaner poem that way, or maybe it accurately denoted some feeling Wordsworth experienced in the moment when he was near the women yet pleasantly alone. Or perhaps it captured a deeper artistic solitude, a separateness partly relieved by the female devotion but also thrown back upon itself. In other words, because they were with him, he could perhaps better tolerate the cosmic loneliness that so frequently accompanies creativity and functions alternately as spur and as impediment.

Or, as he attempted to negotiate the psychological push and pull of conflicting loyalties, he might simply have felt alone among the women. Their mother had died when William was eight, Dorothy six, and early maternal loss often creates a fundamental solitude that can be temporarily relieved but not always transformed.

Whatever feelings permeated his heart's encasement in that moment on the couch, it is clearly thanks to Dorothy's and Mary's devotion that William felt safely alone enough to write poems. Thanks to their love, he could spend time in the solitude of his own mind without feeling anxiously isolated. The psychoanalyst D. W. Winnicott has named this ability "the capacity to be alone with the other," and has noted that its key, paradoxical quality is the way, when you feel secure with another person in your life, nearby but not intruding, you can relax into yourself and let your mind temporarily disorganize in the way it must in order to create.[2] You can let down your guard and turn inward.

The daffodil poem contains silently within it this contradiction between alone and together. However particular in this case to William, the alone/together contradiction is at the core of creative solitude, and it is a large dilemma each art-maker must wrestle in order to keep working.

William and Dorothy, born a year and a half apart, had been separated after their mother's premature death, and they did not see each other at all for nine years, and only intermittently for several more after that. They met again as quasi strangers who shared parents, early memories, and a difficult history of loss and slipshod care. They reconnected with great emotional intensity. Dorothy attached herself to William with the urgency of a very young child refinding a parent—except that she possessed an adolescent's eroticism. And he responded with equal feeling but perhaps an even more complex agenda. Already thinking of himself as a poet, but writing few poems, he sought inspiration as well as stability and succor, and he inhaled her passion and his own as nutrient for his verse-making. Biographer Adam Sisman observed, "sensitive, passionate, and uninhibited, Dorothy acted as a lightning rod for her more reserved brother, showing him flashes of feeling. 'I have thought of you perpetually,' he wrote to her during a walking tour in the Alps, 'and never have my eyes burst upon a scene of particular loveliness but I have instantly wished that you could for a moment be transported to the place where I stood to enjoy it.'" Sisman notes that every morning after the siblings were reunited at Christmas 1790, they "would walk in the garden for two hours, pacing backwards and forwards on the gravel arm in arm, even when the keenest north wind was whistling among the trees, and every evening they would walk another two hours or so, engaged in 'long, long conversation.'"[3]

Describing the relationship around the time of the daffodil walk, Wordsworth's biographer Stephen Gill observes, "Their love for each other was very strong . . . It was domestic. Brother and sister clearly took pleasure in being together all the time—reading, walking digging, building, and planting . . . It was also, unquestionably, profoundly sexual." However, he adds, "Exceptionally intense though it was, it was not exclusive . . . their deepest pleasure was in absorbing others into their intimate life." Across several years, the two seemed to become emotionally one, the poet and his muse /amanuensis merged into a single creature, perceiving the world through one great, curious, alert, and excited Cycloptic eye.[4]

Knowing this background, it would be tempting to hold out that William's claim in "I Wandered Lonely as a Cloud" for solitude as a source of joy and sustenance is false. But that would be way too concrete. After his mother died, the boy sought solace in nature. So his sense of a lonely "self" comforted by rambling in the wild and by contemplating natural beauty provides a true reflection of his feelings. Nature, as he famously declared in his poem "Tintern Abbey," was "the nurse, / The guide, the guardian of [his] heart." It was his poetic and moral inspiration and a great source of pleasure.

Psychologically, it would not be unusual if, after something as huge and crushing as maternal death, his fantasy of nature might become the only place safe enough to entrust some portion of the feelings that otherwise could have flowed to his mother. He speaks elsewhere in "Tintern Abbey" about how nature "Never did betray / The heart that loved her." Certainly, that line expresses a hope. Feeling terrified of letting someone in very close, risking again the immense betrayal of the Grim Reaper's first premature harvest, would seem, for a child, a sensible response to such a devastating loss.

His passion for nature might also have provided a way of diverting other passions, including those for his sister, so that they could remain sublimated enough for him to withstand and transform into poetry rather than consummating them fully—in spite of their intensity, and of his unchaperoned proximity to Dorothy. (Contemporary observers raised eyebrows over the siblings, taking a house together in 1794 and noted their regard for each other, and their unconventional habits of rambling about the hedgerows at all hours, and lying on the hillsides staring at clouds.) In turn, nature glowed brighter for William as his heart became fuller thanks first to his reuniting with Dorothy, and then to his romance with Mary and catalyzing friendship with Samuel Taylor Coleridge. (The latter relationships seem to have been made possible by the greater confidence and security the intense attachment to his sister granted him.) He and Dorothy provided each other with a home, the first true one either had had since their mother died, or arguably before that early loss, since both had been sent to live with relatives for periods even before her death.

William's ability to express himself poetically improved substantially once he was able to draw emotional voltage from Dorothy's devotion. Their mutual engagement worked as a psychic battery that generated power. And the siblings made common cause on his behalf. If he was the cottage rose, she was the trellis that enabled its heavier bloom. One contemporary recalled seeing them walking along during one of their daily outings, William creating and proclaiming lines, Dorothy trailing after, scribbling them in her notebook as she tried to keep pace. Their mixture of separateness and oneness, this emotional arrangement—however we might define it, however we might retrospectively wish for more equality—granted William the strength to better chart out his own sensibility and subjectivity so that he could realize himself as a poet.

For our purposes, the dual narratives of the poem—the man apparently alone, the man actually in intense relationships—and the counterpoint between them underscore how the very concepts of "alone" and "apart" carry psychological complexity. The words are not well served by being reduced to a simple comparison—she was present with him, she was not; they were emotionally merged, they were not. Their meanings are more dynamic and subtle. Yet, to reiterate the paradox: Once William possessed Dorothy so completely, he felt safer in his solitude. We see how he summons her to mind as he hikes through the Alps and every time they are briefly apart. At moments—as with the daffodils—he may have felt peaceful solitude even while in her company, because being near her allowed him to lose himself in contemplation without feeling too lonely. Likely, he did not always experience her as a separate person, but sometimes as a piece of himself that had gone missing, perhaps when his mother died, perhaps not, but one that was now properly restored.

Wordsworth's arrangement also reminds us that the great individual artist is often two different psychological constructions overlaid one upon the other. The first may indeed describe a unique perspective: individual expression, an original response, genius. The second, obvious to all observers yet often discredited or underappreciated, is the surrounding colony of subsumed, often silent contributors, living and dead, who lend support, admiration, inspiration, criticism, enough material and psychological sustenance to enable the artist's development and ongoing expression. How much are they fungible, a bunch of faceless players, logs that simply feed the brilliant flame, and how much particular? William's need for Dorothy seems quite particular. She was kin; she shared the memory of his dead mother and dead father; she wanted to stay with him forever. She knew his distant past—as almost no one else could have. She was also an unusually sensitive and close observer and a perceptive writer. Some have felt that her sensibility was the equal of his, and in his poem "The Sparrow's Nest" (1801), he credits her richly: "She gave me eyes, she gave me ears; / And humble cares, and delicate fears; / A heart, the fountain of sweet tears; / And love, and thought, and joy."[5] It's unclear whether Wordsworth means she put her ears, eyes, and heart in his service, or that she awakened his own. Likely both.

More specifically, I am seeking to remind us how our myth of "the" creative artist working in isolation is just that, and believing it too fully is one way to arrest your own development. Americans continue to have such an extreme fantasy of individuality that we distort emotional reality and misunderstand another essential paradox: Each individual is, of course, unique, and yet each is an ongoing group effort. What you see depends on where you look. We often mistake a front man or woman for a completely separate person. Artists are the voice boxes for colonies of intricately related interdependent creatures, living and dead. No one but Wordsworth could have written Wordsworth's poems, the genius and the primary effort were his, but they only came into being because of webs of collective feeling, labor, memory, and perception that surrounded and permeated him. (At a later point, when Wordsworth was irrationally worried about going to prison for libel, one of the wearied women in his caregiving harem hilariously opined, "We Females . . . have not the least fear of Newgate [prison]—if there was but a Garden to walk in we think we should do very nicely.")[6]

William and Dorothy demonstrate well this contradiction within individuality. Feelings link to other people. Not always a here and now person, but the association is there—in memory, in desire, in the unconscious—somehow. We are psychologically formed, too, first as young children, but progressively throughout our lives, by the way interactions with intimates and the feelings they arouse become not static memories but rather pieces of guiding information, for better and worse, about future encounters with other people. I suspect that one consequence of Dorothy and William's mutual passion was that, like a rain-filled river overflowing its banks, it flooded away the soul-cluttering, inhibiting, unsettling immediacy of the difficult things that had happened to each of them after their parents died; it created a new, fertile landscape; and it provided a mix of distance and closeness that made the past available to be used creatively.

More than simply being guided by the unconscious memories of our emotional experiences with other people, we also carry others around in our minds just the way William took Dorothy with him as he hiked. Often, across time, we internalize many someones with whom we share our sentiments and thoughts. Intensity of feeling heightens that ability, and one reason so many artists repeatedly seek out passionate relationships (whatever the havoc wrought) is so that they can harvest inspiration from the vividness passion grants life and garner support for their work from the fantasy of sharing emotions and experiences with quasi-real, quasi-fantasy, idealized others.

One reason early loss is a psychological experience shared by many artists is not just that it's demographically common (death more so in earlier centuries, but psychological loss prevalent wherever children perceive caretakers as unstable, unsafe, unfocused, or just too long absent). But rather, the experience often leaves children with intense but interrupted feelings that seek outlet and sometimes thus find art. Creativity becomes, psychologically, both a response to the child's real need to be more resourceful than a peer with a mother, and a route to restoring the conversation, the experience of feeling recognized, and the attachment with the departed loved one; thus, it becomes, too, a way of giving expression to rampaging memories and hidden-away feelings that have seemed incommunicable.

Once so deeply connected with Dorothy, William could experience himself as alone with the daffodils, because he felt intact enough to do so. But perhaps he simultaneously felt lonely because he did not know how to tell Dorothy that he wasn't simply marrying Mary pragmatically, but also that he was in love and sexually engaged with her. Maybe he "wandered lonely as a cloud" with Dorothy at his side because he was missing Mary and unable to say so, or because he was worried about how Mary would tolerate, for the long haul, his crucial bond with Dorothy, and he was unable to imagine how he'd work out the ménage. Would both women really stay with him? Could he count on not experiencing another premature and devastating loss? Perhaps having dual loves was one way he hoped to protect himself from future abandonment. Yet again, maybe he was oblivious to these nuances and simply ecstatic because he felt he had just successfully arranged a life of double devotion, no mean feat.

The subjective sense of aloneness can be hard to figure. Most people feel lonely some of the time, and feel unsettling aloneness for periods, and devastating aloneness occasionally, often during grief. But while finding ways to bear our separateness may be our common predicament, it is writ large for people trying to master art-making. In order to tolerate spending lots of time in our minds letting our feelings and thoughts dart about, while still remaining steady enough to harvest solitude's potential riches, it helps greatly if a person possesses a psychological sense of another person's (other people's) benevolent regard for what we are creating. The early death of the Wordsworth children's mother, the emotional absence and premature death of their father, and the indifference of some of their caretakers may have created two psyches that lacked such ballast. And in this sense, the intensity of their passion may have felt like compensation as well as pleasure. It is as if they fused back together something broken. They created one cup from two halves, and each felt better able to dip water from life's well.

Psychological theory aside, emotionally healthy-enough people have different subjective experiences of, and tolerances for, solitude—partly depending on temperament, culture, habit, and circumstance. Throughout life all people experience ups and downs in their sense of separateness and their ability to bear undertakings that demand more of it. These vicissitudes are all part of what artists who work alone have to tolerate. But the important point here is that the long effort of art-making can make people feel dramatically more alone, and more vulnerable, and the severity of that state of empty isolation combined with the heightened vulnerability of creative effort can be one reason people bow out of the process. I am not suggesting you must glom together as the Wordsworths did. But I *am* suggesting that you will be well served to pay close attention to your loneliness, to figure out the psychological and physical companionship you might need. Unless you are in one of those fabulous moments of demonic inspiration where your work takes you over and nothing else matters, how you arrange for all different levels of companionship will greatly inhibit or facilitate your success doing what you set out to do.

Whether you form a peer group, perhaps one in which you critique and support each other's work, or you find a good therapist who understands the complexity of artistic solitude, or you take a workshop every so often, or you just arrange a thrice-weekly coffee or long walk with someone with whom you feel intimate and understood and with whom you can talk deeply about what you're doing (or with whom you can *not* talk about it, as need be), the most important point is to not think that you're better off, or more noble, if you try to go it more completely on your own than is actually right for you.

We look with awe upon groups of great thinkers or artists who came together in the past—the transcendentalists in mid-nineteenth-century Concord, the cubist painters in early twentieth-century Paris, the friendship between Coleridge and Wordsworth, to name only a few of these many pairings and groups. We realize that people seek out each other to find sympathetic spirits. But that's only half the story. The other half is that even when we are not geniuses, our own thinking and creativity are often better catalyzed and stimulated in discourse, not in isolation. We need to work alone; we need to have privacy—sometimes a lot of it—and closing the door and returning to our pens and paper or keyboards or brushes and easels can be bliss; but we also need to be stirred up, stimulated and challenged by others, especially others who share our interests and with whom we feel some modicum of mutual respect.

Wordsworth's genius fed for a while upon Coleridge's. But he likely could take fuller advantage of the relationship because he had Dorothy and Mary in his corner to help buffer him from the competitive challenges of conversation with another brilliant poet. Indeed, the confirming and motivating feelings that come from friendships with other artists are accompanied by other feelings that can be neither predictable nor easily tolerable, so it helps to have ways of soothing the resulting scrapes. If you read Evan Hughes's portrait of the loose web of late-twentieth-century friendships that included Jonathan Franzen, Mary Karr, Jeffrey Eugenides, and David Foster Wallace, you can see clearly how much the writers were both mutually admiring and fiercely competitive rivals. While they could offer generous praise, they could also be deeply critical of each other's work.[7] I imagine that after spending time together, each of them sometimes fled home to write in private, not aglow with warm inspiration, but more the way World War I soldiers hunkered down in the trenches: to dodge the blows from the others' opinions and books so that they could write their own, which they hoped would explode with even more brightness than the ones lobbed over their heads. Or, failing to triumph, they struggled to write books good enough to keep them from feeling "one down" from the others in this circle. They carried each other into solitude as friends, but perhaps even more as creative goads. It seems they were often invaluable to each other in this capacity, but I imagine they could use each other most effectively, if, like Wordsworth, they had other relationships that offered more support and buffer.

THERE ARE TIMES when the art-maker's solitude feels mildly pleasant, or deeply pleasurable, or even blissful. Many people refer to Mihaly Czikszentmihalyi's concept of "flow" as their experience of art-making—that state of being in which one is focused and concentrated, removed from time, energized, and not lonely at all. But flow happens most readily when the task is not too frustrating, and when the obstacles feel manageable. I feel flow when the writing is going well more readily than when I'm trying to wrangle with some thorny bit of it. Then I feel unflow and, sometimes, too alone with the labor and very glad to have fond people close at hand in my life and in my memory.

At its worst, the aloneness of the art-maker's effort can feel virulent. To illustrate this nastiness, let us imagine someone like Dorothy separated from William and Mary, as a young contemporary artist who has removed herself to her Brooklyn garret while they linger in the Lake District.

What are the components of this more vertiginous experience? When I seriously pursue the fantasy, I immediately come up against the reality that Dorothy knew how to support William's creative work more readily than she knew how to support her own. So, Dorothy's first difficulty would be in allowing herself to not immediately yield to her guilt at turning her attention away from her brother. I mention this thought because so many— women particularly, though some men, too—never manage to stay in their work because their delight in making use of their own creative solitude immediately gets drowned in the guilt and sometimes shame they feel about even temporarily abandoning their role of serving or caring for others. Furthermore, in this rearranged contemporary trio, William may be so absorbed in himself, and Mary so absorbed in William, that Dorothy may set about her labor without a sense of having others with her in a way that actually supports her efforts, a problem she might have to address both inside herself and then with firm words to William. But, setting aside this likelihood, let us have her continue on.

Someone working seriously usually seeks quiet to facilitate concentration, so she sets herself apart from others physically. Furthermore, each time she enters the studio or study, she does not simply separate herself, but also signs on to do mental spelunking. She becomes like an archaeologist searching for cave paintings.

Something about the area and the features of the land, together with stories she's heard, suggests to her that they are nearby, but she has no sure knowledge that they exist in any one locale. She agrees to spend hours in her own mind delving deep, crawling through dark, dank passages squinting into gloom, thinking and feeling hard, all the while unable to raise her head for fear of bumping it as she searches. By which I mean she has signed on to explore her memories and sensations, her thoughts, her impressions. She is attempting to bring into the world something partially visualized but unseen and not yet known even to her.

Sometimes, she is happily carried along by her curiosity, engagement, and interest. She is relieved to be out from under William's and Mary's gaze, however loving, because she enjoys the privacy and the freedom to escape their opinions and general nattering, or even their familiar definitions of her. She is excited by her pursuit, and by her passage through the tangled labyrinth. Other times, making her way through such a mental space becomes laborious, and that effort separates her further psychologically from succor than the closed door has separated her physically. No intimate is actually beside her offering cheer, joining minds with her, cocreating the musical notes, or dialogues, or painted images. So her thoughts wobble between being shared in fantasy with someone whose company she imagines or inchoately senses and being felt as hers and hers only. And that latter singularity is both the much-touted essence of the undertaking and the source of a sometimes torturous isolation.

Without putting too fine a point on it, if Dorothy is here, and they are in the Lake District, and at the end of the workday when she sits to read, or watches a DVD, and her doubts assail her, even with all the help offered by Skype, texting, and email, a glass of bourbon with new neighbors, she remains remarkably more isolated and thus vulnerable to having her doubts arrest her than William ever was.

Let me digress a bit here to briefly consider the "new media" and some of the ways it affects the dilemma of solitude I've been describing. Many people, including me, attempt to regulate their solitude using email, texting, or the Internet, and there are pros and cons to the effort. I find this new technology most useful when heavily supplemented with face time with real friends and intimates. Here's why: Solitude and isolation are very close states of being, but with very different psychological feelings. Solitude is time in one's own mind that feels manageable and often pleasurable; people use it for introspection of different kinds—fantasizing, mulling over problems, planning, meditating. Isolation is unchosen separateness, which creates a sense of undesired aloneness, and it tends to make people feel itchy, restless, even panicky, empty or gray inside, and it tends to shut down, preoccupy, or cloud the mind. I find that too much time using the computer to help me manage solitude can lead me into all the negative feelings of isolation—and they can take me over without my even realizing what's happened. I know from listening to friends and patients that my experience is widely shared.

Email, texting, Facebook, Twitter, and Skype, to name but the most common of the endlessly expanding variations of contemporary communication, are each different. But they have the so-obvious-we-forget-it's-dumbfounding feature of letting us communicate in real time, or something close to it, with people who are not remotely in our physical presence. We've had messengers carrying messages for millennia, and letters (which we will talk about in the next chapter) have existed for centuries; the telegraph is over 150 years old, and telephones started ringing across New York City and other parts of the urbanized world before the twentieth century commenced. So what's different now? The radically altered proportion of non–face-to-face time in a person's day. It's staggeringly different. And the possibilities it opens up are fabulous—and thrilling. But, human-to-human communication hasn't traditionally included just words or images. It's been a whole-body affair. And, while we have gained plenty with the new media, we seem also to be creating a system of virtual "being there" in which the cumulative impact of sensory deprivation is significant even as it's overlooked. I'm not certain. The changes are too new and ongoing to be easily understood.

But here's why we need to watch carefully: This sensory deprivation may be part of what turns solitude into weird, bad-feeling isolation when you spend too much time with social media. Until well into this century, people communicated almost exclusively with others who were at their side, or on their street, or in their workplace. They looked at, touched, and smelled each other. They watched the endless array of subtle facial gestures made by the other person's eyes, lips, forehead, and nose. They noticed cheeks flushing or growing pale. They felt the heat off the other person's body, the smell of wet wool when someone came in from the damp; they heard coughs or labored breathing. They sniffed perfume or sweat or yesterday's gin or pheromones or garlic on the breath. They nodded, they snarled, they shook a fist or delivered a cuff to the head. But they also undid a badly chosen word with a touch on the arm; they met distress—or calamitous grief—with an embrace. Emotion grew from this whole array of sensations. And emotions are what make people feel alive and in their bodies.

I'm not claiming all this up-close contact always made people feel better. In fact, when you seek solitude, you relish the absence of exactly these stimuli; you relish being free of other people and their damn emotions. And nowadays you can shield yourself as you never could before. If you are writing (or relaxing after working on another creative enterprise), you can sit at your computer with your headphones on, listening to music, and when you get stuck or feel lonely, you can check your email, or visit Facebook, or read some news on the web and feel slightly reconnected and as if you're in a comfortable, warm little space that lets you enter and leave your work according to your own needs undisturbed.

However, if we overly "screen" ourselves, if we set ourselves apart from other people more than occasionally, we not only become too precious and picky, not to mention chronically undersocialized, but also too remote, and too ungrounded. We become gated communities of one. Emotions get more narrowly communicated. Experience loses dimension and texture. We don't get enough stimulation from others to power our own batteries (or give enough to power theirs). And we can fall into a kind of detached mental vagueness or ennui that lacks adequate vivacity and vividness to truly sustain us—or our work.

We know, for instance, that as well as the other tactile stimulation I described, mutual physiological regulation occurs when you're physically with friends or intimates. Your breathing slows, your stress hormones lower, you settle. Or, conversely, your metabolism picks up, you chat and feel stimulated, or laugh and feel elated. There's no doubt you can feel some bit of these types of shifts and their relief when you make contact over email or Facebook. But my impression is that it tends to be of shorter duration and less depth. It keeps fading, and you keep needing another hit. And because each new bit of email (or phone texting) or news offers this slight stimulant shot to the brain, it's too easy to become like the rat tapping the lever to get a further dose of drug. You think you are behaving rationally or at least you are rationalizing the increasing pace of self-interruption. But really, you are not concentrating deeply anymore. (This problem is so widespread that people are using Internet programs to turn off their access to email and the Internet for various lengths of time.)

Nor can social media effectively regulate self-critical mental processes. People often talk to me about conversations they have with themselves in their head, a universal phenomenon. But since efforts to master or create tend to raise up critical voices, the muted or superficial discourse online is often not enough to really soothe or quiet them the way conversation with another real and present person can. Your head can become an echo chamber, answered by you, but not actually tempered by another person. A recent study lends evidence to my assertion: When researchers studied stress hormone levels in distressed daughters who either telephoned or texted with their mothers, only the ones who heard their mothers' voices on the telephone felt better, and had a rise in oxytocin, the hormone that signals comforted feelings, and a lowering of cortisol, the stress hormone.[8]

A further peril of regulating solitude too exclusively through social media is that it's really easy online to come upon too much information—and get more stressed even as you're seeking solace, or relief from isolation. If Dorothy in Brooklyn, feeling lonely, goes to William's Facebook page to see what he's up to, she may get a dose of feeling contact with him, but it's likely to be much less encompassing than if they were together. And what if she reads his post that he is having a happy time, perhaps a happier time, with Mary and S. Coleridge when she is absent? Or what if she learns that they are pulling together a pamphlet that ignores her recent work? It isn't that she wouldn't have had plenty of similar opportunities to feel rebuffed in person (and she had her difficult moments), but she and the others would all have shared the same physical space—rather than merely the virtual space where she has become the voyeuristic and helpless onlooker. We don't know, but my view is that where mood regulation and solitude are concerned, reentering the real fray is more likely to lead to better and worse feelings, but ones you can deal with and resolve and that are less likely to create the more ruminative, negative, low-grade, bland sense of quasi emptiness that too much screen time and physical distance sometimes create.

II

RETURNING AGAIN TO the daffodils, Wordsworth's claim of solitude in the midst of proximity also sheds light on how the meaning of the word has evolved considerably since the early nineteenth century, when it applied more to a mental state of reverie or briefer separations, or life in a cottage of friends away from the city, and less to situations of prolonged physical separateness. (For William, "solitude" often meant composing while walking back and forth outdoors in the garden so that no one would break his concentration, even as he stayed nearby.) This evolution sheds light on our current confusion. Today physical separateness is the essential association we have with the idea.

William's need was not so much for a room, but for a space in which he could be mentally with himself enough to write, yet not psychologically too alone to mute his wish to write. And the reason we have lingered with the Wordsworths is that in their fashion they solved the problem of artistic solitude—at least for William. Artists need different mixes of psychological and physical space to create the balance of alone and together that best serves their effort of expression. Meanwhile, the arrangements that work creatively may not be perfect domestically in other ways. Yet too many people today who wish to master a craft or art form carry a notion of solitude that is, as I said earlier, way too solitudinous. They seek to stay alone longer than is good for them.

Indeed, contemporary Americans tend to forget, or simply not to know, how unusual physical solitude has been in human history. Until the past few hundred years, the occasional hermit or mystic might have lived apart from the group, but only recently has the studio apartment been deemed a good idea. Researching my first book, *Private Matters*, I learned that in seventeenth-century Connecticut, to cite one example, it was illegal to live alone. And, if other colonies lacked a similar law, it was likely because the desire itself was considered unusual enough to make legislation unnecessary. Humans have tended to run in packs, and by and large even curmudgeonly, introverted psyches have sought some sociability. Today, although Americans are physically solitary when measured against the past, research suggests more contact than we might expect. A contemporary report sums up, "People are social by nature, spending about 80% of their waking hours with family, friends, or co-workers."[9]

My guess—completely not evidence-based—is that if one had measured the prevalence of physical solitude across past cultures and centuries, until maybe one hundred years ago in America and Western Europe, most male artists and artisans would have lived and even labored in the immediate company of other people about 98 percent of the time. For women, the figure would have crept up toward 99.9 percent.

Now, conventions of contemporary art-making (i.e., solitary travail) require that practitioners defy the current 80/20 split and spend considerably more hours apart from others. What's more, our cultural image of "alone" is represented narrowly as "no one else around" for much of the day.

We partly cling to the worth of extreme separateness because we've been told that strong people favor it, but also partly in an effort to manage the psychological quandary we touched on before: Companionship is invaluable when, psychologically, you are surrounded by nonintrusive or self-sacrificing or admiring others, whose purpose is to make your creative existence better, but it is more distracting, oppressive, and irritating if you are trying to write some verse of your own and waiting (in your unconscious mind) for the next call to serve, complaint, or criticism. While there's no easy out to that predicament, being aware of the dilemma is the first step to making a more conscious decision about how much to yield to its command.

While artists may tend toward introversion, and some may possess pleasure in physical distance, novices are often unprepared for how difficult the self-imposed separation can feel. And not just novices; I remember a story about an accomplished poet—a married man with several children—who'd been granted a month's stay at an artists' colony. Upon arrival he was assigned to an airy room at the top of a big old mansion. The housemistress climbed the stairs with him, showed him to his studio, recited a list of amenities and rules, and departed. The poet opened the suitcase and unpacked his pencil and pad. He sat down at the desk. He stood up. Making his way around the room, he peered out through all the window panes. He contemplated the treetops above, and the expansive lawn below. He sighed. Then he closed his suitcase, clunked it down the stairs, and mumbled a quick but definitive good-bye to the nonplused matron. Rather than sanctuary, the tree house room delivered a wallop of anxiety and isolation. Perhaps he, unlike many who relish their time in artists' colonies, could only bear the poet's solitude at home when his wife and children went about their lives in nearby rooms.

So we seek to avoid the unpleasant invasiveness and unwanted, oppressive influence of other people, the voices that scold, demean, or too harshly challenge us, and yet—as I mentioned when discussing social media—the mind often preserves equilibrium better when its own excesses are continually interrupted. The Puritans in colonial New England rejected solitude because it enabled communion with the devil. They sagely grasped that folks quickly become weird when not surrounded and chatted up. Sit in your mountaintop for a few days without company, and how the mind does begin to cut loose and meander. You can blame Lucifer or not, but odd things happen: visions; night dreams during daylight hours; decapitated, otherworldly voices having their say; one's own voice speaking aloud to no one in particular; intense fear; heightened sexuality; out-of-body feelings; more anxiety and depression—you name it.

Without other people, there exists no external counterforce to arrest solipsistic drift, nor any barrier to restrain ruminative excess. The whirlpool in one's head foams away too much energy. Ideas, often bad ones, take on a life of their own. And emotions spin about wildly without either nets to catch them or surfaces to deflect and channel them. Close company provides a check to perseverating unrealities. And more than that, as the Wordsworths so ably demonstrate, even in the kinkier situations, when the groupthink seems a tad bizarre, cottagemates can still provide intense feeling, emotional richness, stimulating companionship, and loyal friendship.[10]

Thanks in part to misconception lingering from Romanticism, indeed from Wordsworth's very daffodils, we hold a distorted notion that our feelings and creative impulses need to be only ours and harvested by us in isolation. But the reality is richer, more paradoxical, more peculiar, and less within our willful control. Simply put, to sustain the effort of art-making, it helps to have a sense, felt more than thought—sometimes eroticized, sometimes not—of someone, or several, who stay(s) near you in your mind, and who is interested in you and in what you have to say. Such fantasies are ubiquitous parts of mental life, hardly only the domain of artists. But the difference for art-makers is that they particularly need to arrange a balance that stimulates their creativity yet supports their solitude.

We all need ongoing real emotional contact and varied sources of emotional voltage to continue working. Devotion on the extraordinary level of Dorothy's and Mary's (and Coleridge's) for William is unusual. Genius is a potent draw. Most of us make do with much less. We may simply speak in our minds to a beloved person and look forward to seeing our spouse or children or a friend at the end of the day. Often the mental conversation is not with a particular person, but rather a vaguer, more fluid, and preconscious sensation. Over years, if we are fortunate, a large pile of mental images or memories—old friends, kind words from intimates, mentors' instructions and praise, the memory of small or large successes—accumulates and banks around us, tempering negative feelings and insulating the mind against too-frequent encounters with its own devastating state of solitary confinement.

CHAPTER 6

identity

I

ALMOST 150 YEARS after Wordsworth wrote about the daffodils, the poets Robert Lowell and Elizabeth Bishop began to write each other letters. *Words in Air*, an eight-hundred-page volume of their twenty-eight-year correspondence, records another variation in the ways artists use close relationships in the service of their art-making, particularly, in this case, giving credibility to and supporting their identities as poets. Their correspondence also reveals how they encouraged each other and lent crucial support to each other's art-making. The take-home *Pilgrim's Progress* lesson is that even when you have a primary intimacy, you still need to find other sources of encouragement and support that help you feel legitimate in what you are doing.

The absence of this kind of stimulation, this reminder of the worth of your art-making identity, is an important reason people become demoralized and stop trying. But, as Lowell and Bishop demonstrate, creating a stable relationship that sustains both parties is itself a delicate and complex mission.

Lowell and Bishop first met, notes Dan Chiasson in a *New Yorker* piece about the correspondence,

> *in 1947 at a dinner party thrown by Randall Jarrell in New York. Bishop recalled, "It was the first time I had ever talked to some one about how one writes poetry." She found that talking with Lowell, who struck her as "handsome in an old-fashioned poetic way," was strangely easy, "like exchanging recipes for a cake." It had been a strange, lonely interval for them both. Lowell was twenty-nine and coming out of his disastrous first marriage to the novelist Jean Stafford. (Stafford had sued him, before they were married, after he permanently injured her face in a car crash. Things went downhill from there.) Bishop was turning thirty-six, and her relationship with Marjorie Stevens, from Key West, was coming to an end.*[1]

BISHOP HAD BEGUN writing poems in high school and had co-founded a literary magazine while at Vassar. She'd maintained a long, important friendship with the poet Marianne Moore, so it is more than a little striking to hear her comment that her conversation with Lowell was her first about the "how" of writing poetry. Yet the two quickly became fast friends, and it's hard to imagine that their easy, engaged conversation about their common work wasn't key. Certainly the letters suggest it was. Lowell and Bishop also shared the birthplace of Massachusetts and a passion for the Maine coast. They were both sharp-eyed, witty observers; both great readers of literature and poetry, appreciators of music; both epic consumers of alcohol, plagued by terrible depression (alternating, in Lowell's case, with mania).

And they were both shaped by tough childhoods, simultaneously privileged and deprived, which left them permanently uncentered and easily tipped. They were like two great, injured sea turtles in a roiled sea, often flipped over, upended, having to right themselves enough to struggle along. They visited in person for a few days every few years. But mostly, from 1948 until Lowell's death in 1977, they corresponded. While they often lived far away from each other, there were also psychological and artistic reasons they built and maintained their friendship by writing more than talking, and it is the latter I wish to plumb here. Their arrangement helps us understand more about the way relationships assist people in sustaining their "artist" identities. Unlike the Wordsworths, these two friends were most useful to each other, and apparently happiest in their relationship, when they were apart and writing letters. Also unlike the Wordsworths, they appreciated each other as equals.

Letters, now quickly becoming historical relics, are odd and remarkable human productions. Their mundane surface, their casual labor bridging distance and delivering news, belies their extraordinary ability to grasp a moment in an individual's mind and to lay out upon a page unrivaled views both of the speaker's soul or psyche and of his surroundings. On April 24, 1952, Lowell, in Holland with his second wife, Elizabeth Hardwick, writes Bishop about how their apartment is full of half-packed suitcases, the trees outside the window are leafing, the sun is bright, Mozart is playing on the radio, "and each of us knows that if he can only stall long enough the other will do the packing. Our long green coffin-like trunk that we counted on to hold almost everything is brimful of books."[2]

In two sentences, Lowell offers up a vivid sense of an April moment that is at once a beginning and an ending, an evocation of lassitude, of impending departure, of the familiar hope that one's partner will leave her chair first to shoulder the effort the situation demands. He also offers, through his phrasing and careful images, a snapshot of himself as a poet.

Though they may be quickly scribbled and animatedly received, once the present moment passes, the content of letters comes to resemble time in a still life, at once static and dynamic, inanimate before the eye, and yet evoking immediate actions that will or have occurred "offstage." No dinner guest is present. There is only the meal to come or its residue—the oysters open and ready to be consumed, or the empty shells and squeezed-out lemon rinds on the platter waiting to be cleared. As with the still life, the letter's spontaneity before the viewer is the result not simply of the painter's brush but also of her care in setting up the objects and studying them. And letters, though they may convey great freshness in their detail, often include some of the self-conscious, or unconscious, selectivity and contrivance of a scene arranged for painting.

Lowell and Bishop use letters to keep each other company, develop a friendship, comment on each other's verse, and to clarify for themselves aspects of their literary efforts. They also use them to confirm and embolden their identities as poets. You cannot write a letter any more than you can paint a self-portrait without choosing a profile. You might not think about it much as you rearrange your head until it seems right, but you do it. And the profile each needed to find in the other's mirror is of himself or herself as a credible artist. Who besides a fellow writer would really appreciate Lowell's trunk too quickly brimful of books? So much of their correspondence, beneath the quotidian reporting, is a relentless reiteration of identity, a performative utterance (in other words, an action in the form of speech) presented by detailing the artist's arsenal. You can see I am a poet because my trunk, an object that for most people holds clothing, is brimful of books. "The long green coffin-like trunk" could easily initiate a Lowell stanza. There is the shared pleasure of finding another like yourself who can appreciate how trunks get too filled with books. The two assumed each other as audience in a way that allowed them to rehearse themselves as well as the literary aspects of their lives. Their exchange helped them amass, support, and secure the identity of "poet" and gave good weight to a labor in a country whose bards often feel as consequent as tumbleweeds.

Lowell and Bishop were both ambitious, talented writers dedicated to their vocation. In 1948, Lowell wrote Bishop, "Sometimes nothing is solid to me as writing. I suppose that's what vocation means—at times a torment, a bad conscience, but all in all, purpose and direction, so I'm thankful and call it good."[3] If, as Lowell postulates, nothing is as solid to you as writing (a nice encapsulation of the paradox of the artist's state), you are at once at work and in trouble, since the labor of art's production is as effortful as it is invisible. The letters sought to make it visible, as much to the writers as to the recipients, to concretize it so it could bear weight.

On December 12, 1958, Lowell wrote that he had completed a book and consequently passed the winter in "joyful dissipation."[4] He lists a paragraph of books he's been reading—from Chekhov to Tolstoy to Dostoyevsky, Hawthorne, Fitzgerald, James, Lawrence, Melville. He describes seeing ballets in Manhattan and dining with Mary McCarthy and W. H. Auden. He enjoys recounting a good time in the city; he also wants Bishop to witness him living the literary life. He wants to remind her and himself that such a life is exciting and credible, and that they share it and support each other in it. In theory, he could write that letter to any friend, but my guess is that he felt that her informed witness would be more appreciative. As he relived the hours and then put details on paper, he could imagine her understanding why the events felt meaningful.

Bishop, in turn, confirms that the letters serve a similar function for her when she writes, "Dearest Cal: Please never stop writing me letters—they always manage to make me feel like my higher self."[5] Her reference to a higher self a la Emerson is tongue-in-cheek, and yet it's serious. Lowell has seen the part of herself she finds bearable, even a source of pride, not disgusting to her, not alien. He had written, "You are about the only poet now who calls her own tune."[6] He has read her new poems—always a moment of peril for an artist—and he mirrors her writer "self" back to her as original. He goes on to compare her favorably to Marianne Moore and Ezra Pound, two of the living best.

At the same time, he offers her a few ideas about things she might improve, moving the poem more toward a dramatic monologue, and suggesting that if she revises, she should add some line. His praise is more credible for being modulated; his criticism, from a fellow practitioner, likely useful. It's very hard to improve beyond a point without frequently showing your work to people who possess some authority in the area in which you're laboring, and who you feel can judge it intelligently and yet name its weaknesses. Such vulnerable revelation is easier to manage both when you hold a full sense of its necessity, and when you trust the other person.

And as is so important to such artistic/critical camaraderie, Lowell and Bishop each trusts that the other possesses a *sympatique* sensibility. He has made clear that he admires her. She has confirmed that she admires him. The security that springs from the mutual appreciation—specifically the praise by an esteemed fellow artist—encourages both to voice themselves more fully in their work. This cycle of risk and confirmation between people who respect each other's standards and talent is the photosynthesis of artistic confidence, the sun and chlorophyll that let something grow seemingly from nothing. (If we think of what waylays our pilgrim's progress, one peril is a poorly chosen comrade who undermines or continually grates away at our confidence, who refuses to substantiate our identity.)

For Lowell and Bishop, the choice of communicating through letters is more than a simple convenience. The space between them grants them more freedom about what they tell. Sometimes that distance creates fuller expression and greater frankness; other times it allows larger omissions. You can describe your higher self and thus lay a plank across your horror at the other parts of you that may impede. This "planking" is crucial. They sometimes confide their troubles. But, aided by the distance, they do not criticize each other for repeated missteps, boozing, and crack-ups. They listen, and then choose to speak about what the other does well.

After a silence Bishop has found worrisome, Lowell finally writes her. Between the lines, you get a sense that illness, distraction, and shame have caused him to eschew communicating: "I was in the hospital for five weeks or so . . . Once more there was a girl, rather a foolish girl but full of a kind of life and earth force, and once more a great grayness and debris left behind me at home." All but the last page of Bishop's response is lost, but what's left suggests she is as usual more newsy than intrusive. She understands his effort to mop up a mess, and she tells him she's just happy to hear that he's better. Such expressions of support go both ways. Encouraging her to look up Philip Larkin and several other poets while she's in England, he assures her that they will welcome her warmly and that they admire her work.[7]

As with many close friendships, theirs included loyalty, practical assistance (Lowell, who had more early success, worked hard advancing Bishop's career and found jobs and other opportunities for her), observations (sometimes delightfully catty) about friends held in common, literary news, accounts of their doings, and updates on family members. But what made theirs an artists' friendship was not simply the practical assistance, nor the number of useful and supportive comments they made about each other's art, but the way they psychologically positioned themselves. In the photo on the book jacket, the two stand each with a single arm upon the other's shoulder. Their bodies are slightly angled in, and their eyes meet fondly. Bishop is diminutive and birdlike, so short that she must tip back her head to find his gaze; Lowell, lanky, tall, in dark-framed glasses, bends his head down to meet her. Their stance is evocative of the way soccer players link arms to guard their goal. Poets—certainly in America—often must struggle to defend their chosen career. The effort to stay beside oneself can be exhausting. But when another person stands with you, the capacity for defense becomes twice as robust. The letters served as a way of holding that stance.

But why letters? The telephone was ubiquitous in urban postwar America. The poets Anne Sexton and Maxine Kumin famously used to telephone each other and work for hours composing verses, each with her phone beside her so that she might try out a phrase or line or just seek sustenance from the other without even having to redial. (When one wanted the other's attention, she whistled into the receiver.)[8] Yet Lowell and Bishop often preferred to convey their news in writing even when they were on the same continent. Why? Well for one reason, letters grant each participant more control (especially in an era before answering machines). Calling brings the other person to your side. You cannot see her or touch her, but, for better or worse, she is speaking in your ear. You ring her up when you think of her and wish to speak with her. But she might be irritated to have her rhyming interrupted; she might be drunk. You might be a little manic and in the mood to pick a fight. You might state your opinions too forcefully in that overbearing way you sometimes have. It could become unpleasant.

Letters generally present a more complex (or disjointed) sense of distance. The conversation does not occur in real time. Both the reader and the writer can control the pace of contact and can modulate the emotions and feeling states—like competition, influence, envy, aggression, passion, or anger. The reader can read a line and put down the paper, or rush through the paragraphs and then repeatedly reread chosen parts. The writer can write and rewrite, begin, pause, edit, and begin again. Each can be alone with his or her thoughts and feelings and choose more deliberately which to share. You may feel breathlessly close reading the proffered sentiments, anecdotes, and opinions, or you can feel overwhelmed by rage or envy, but in either case you are reading and you are apart. You have time to settle your feathers before you reply.

I want to underscore this "apart" dimension because I'm explicitly attempting to grab and name a subjective experience of "being apart" that in its turn provokes a wish to reach out to someone absent. Earlier, writing about Keats, I traced out the notion that art-making includes within it a longing to reunite with someone who has been lost. I revisit another aspect of that notion later in this chapter. Meanwhile, I want to capture another nuance of the unconscious dimension of creative effort and companionship. With Keats, I was focused on one of the psychological intentions behind his impulse to write. Here, I am describing something about how the longing to communicate with someone "not here" can function as a profoundly steadying force—a walking stick, improving balance as one traverses rocky places—firming the artist's identity, sustaining the effort and the excitement, and diminishing isolation while he or she makes the art.

In this variation, the other person seems not so much dead or permanently lost, but alive and away. Perhaps on a voyage. The motif is absence. Probably you are bartering with finality—with forever—but that's left ambiguous. You are aware of the absence of the other. At the same time, the other is present by being absent and yet held in awareness. Sometimes sharply, other times quietly, the subjective experience can be particular, but it is often a little inchoate or preconscious—drifting in and out of mind— a sense that one's heart is lightly but warmly cupped. Stepping away now from the molten needs of Dorothy and William, the urge here is more for companionship, friendship, maybe at moments intense, occasionally erotically tinged, but mostly more peacefully loving, and thus, overall, less about passionate, romantic reuniting. In this instance, the optimal distance of creative companionship is a surround, an atmosphere within one's own mind created by a sense of another who is present in her absence.

In a 1954 letter, Lowell wrote to Elizabeth, who was then living in Brazil. He asks her if she'll stop in to see them on her way to Europe: "I wish with all my heart that you could somehow stretch things and see us. We seem attached to each other by some stiff piece of wire, so that each time one moves, the other moves in another direction."[9] I'm not certain of Lowell's own interpretation of the jerking oppositeness he describes, and he does not say. But a reader of their correspondence might conclude that avoiding too much face time was the point. They wanted and needed some, but not too much. To be most useful, they had to be apart, with space and motivation to describe their lives, while sometimes vaguely other times more intensely longing to be together. They each found it creatively stimulating and sustaining to engage with someone who existed not here but elsewhere. This distance created the missing other as audience for each one's self-presentation and work. Letter writing served as a way not just to communicate with a friend, but—almost like a perfume atomizer—as a way to revivify the atmosphere with the other's presence, to heighten it just enough so that it would remain vaguely with you while you went about your day's art-making. On June 7, 1956, Bishop writes, "Dearest Cal, I don't know why I've been so slow about writing to you, since I think of you every day of my life I'm sure." On August 7, 1961, Lowell writes, "My Dearest Elizabeth: The other night I had a dream about you . . . Somewhere on the edges you were, but we couldn't come together, and all was a headache of difficulties and distances."[10]

Letter writing forces you as letter writer to bring thoughts and feelings into awareness. While the act superficially resembles something that would occur in conversation, because the recipient is more distant, the process is more private, and more particular. The self-expression paces itself differently from conversation and adopts different emphases. In letter writing you tell yourself the narrative in the presence of the fantasy other; the actual flesh-and-blood living recipient reads it later. The time lapse protracts the contact—writing, waiting, hearing back. And because the recipient is at a distance, his or her capacities are more easily bent a little by you so as to better fit your wishes. The distance allows you to enhance the human qualities you need in a companion to help your work proceed and develop. You half intuit, half assume how *that* person will understand your effort well, perhaps better than anyone who is at hand. And that perception might be a wish, or it might be a fact. You have a second person with whom to hold an emotion, but that person is not too present and disruptive.

Bishop was already thirty-six before she met someone with whom she was comfortable talking about her craft. Many artists feel profoundly isolated in their everyday surroundings. So, another function of letters is to allow an artist to build a community—across space—of fellow laborers. On August 26, 1963, Bishop wrote to Lowell, "Virgil T says 'one of the strange things about poets is the way they keep warm by writing to one another all over the world.'"[11]

You want to tune your own mental radio so that it finds the broadcast frequency you seek. To facilitate your own work, you need a particular response, or a specific emotion commonly held, and at times the acceptable bandwidth is narrow. There may only be one station far away that plays your songs. Bishop wanted to talk craft with Lowell, but she also felt overwhelmed by him, especially during his manic bouts. People in the flesh—where your artistic "self" is involved—may create too much static. They may dominate or discourage you. (Coleridge admired Wordsworth way too much, and at his own expense. He sometimes could only see Wordsworth's genius when they were together, not his own. Conversely, there were periods when Wordsworth felt lost without Coleridge's comments on his work and guidance about direction.) To facilitate your effort, you seek psychological audience with someone who does not intrude too much, who lets you metabolize him or her as your creative need dictates.

Yet the letter recipient, the other person, is not attractive to you for being malleable nor a creation of your imagination. Quite the contrary. He or she satisfies the human need for "original response"—as Robert Frost once put it. In fact, Frost's poem "The Most of It" humorously touches exactly on that relational complexity when he presents his lonely alter ego shouting across a lake and hoping to hear "original response" rather than merely the echo of his own voice. In Frost's tongue-in-cheek vision, when the wished-for stranger finally appears, he turns out not to be a comprehending human but a large moose crashing through the underbrush. Yet the implied overlay of echo and "other" is a psychologically apt way of describing a correspondent. You know and love real things about the other person. She says what she has to say, not what you would make her say. At the same time, because of the distance, and because you have granted her a place in your imagination, there's a way that her originality, rather than being difficult, is both critically useful and also confirming of the worth of your shared endeavor, often seeming to echo and highlight that which is dearest to you.

Letters also allow two people to be very dear to each other without ruffling their lives over it. They can enjoy intimate feelings without acting on them. This on-paper intimacy is another way of creating a warm fire against the chill of solitudinous effort.

A lovely telling of the contradictory wish of "with me and apart" is laid out in a very long, oft-quoted letter Lowell wrote Bishop in 1957. She, together with her Brazilian lover, Lota (Maria Carlota Costallat de Macedo Soares), had recently visited him and his wife, Elizabeth—called Lizzie—in Castine, Maine. At some point during the visit Lowell had suggested to Bishop that they meet up and spend time alone. Bishop reported the conversation to Lizzie. His overture and his mental state disturbed her, and she and Lota departed sooner than they had planned. Lowell, though becoming manically ill, was self-aware enough still to feel distressed, and he writes apologetically that "My disease, alas, gives one (during its seizures) a headless heart." She sends him back a newsy letter implying indirectly that she has not taken umbrage, and he begins the lengthy, famous August 15 letter by expressing his "terrific relief" and allowing, "I feared that I was forever in exile."[12]

And it seems the threat of loss ups Lowell's urgency for attachment. A few pages later, he writes, "Do you remember how at the end of that long swimming and sunning Stonington day . . . we were talking about this and that . . . But at the time everything, I guess (I don't want to overdramatize) our relations seemed to have reached a new place. I assumed that would be just a matter of time before I proposed and I half believed that you would accept." Lowell continues, describing the way that he wanted to pick the right moment to ask her to wed him, but somehow there were a series of wrong moments. He describes another occasion, when he is drunk and cold: "and I felt half-dying and held your hand. And nothing was said, and like a loon that needs sixty feet I believe, to take off from the water, I wanted time and space . . . I was determined to ask you." He does not ask her to marry him, and in the letter he muses, "But asking you is *the* might have been for me, the one towering change, the other life that might have been."[13]

The other life that might have been. We pass this way once, and we can often perceive vividly, heartbreakingly, other paths we might have taken. (At the same time, the phrase also offers a definition of art's own space, exemplified by Minor White and Abe Frajndlich, as a death-defying place of play and reconsideration.) Lowell's comment contains a genuine recognition of love and a genuine wish. He wants to marry her; he wants to try to temper her loneliness. Yet he chooses to confess to Bishop at a time when she has just visited with her own beloved in tow. Perhaps her passionate pairing with Lota made him jealous, made him urgent, made him feel he was losing her, or woke up other losses and abandonments. But it could also have made her safer as a person apart, so he could long for her more openly without feeling any danger that she would actually move toward him. She, in turn, holding steady in this distance and yet allowing him to feel filled with longing, assured that their friendship would continue. Her letter back to him is mostly newsy but begins with a suggestion, seemingly following upon a conversation they had in Maine, that he consult with Lota's ex-psychoanalyst next time he's in Cambridge. Toward the end she gently offers, "I do hope you're feeling much, much better, Cal."[14] Lowell sometimes expresses sexual interest in Bishop, which Bishop appears not to have returned. People describe the experience of mania as hypersexualized or at least akin to the hyperaliveness of sexual passion and romantic love but less in control and more likely to go off the rails. So it's hard to know what to make of his telling her of his desire, an ambiguity complicated further by his knowledge that Bishop's sexual love is for women.

II

ARTISTS SEEK TO express deep emotions and to capture what feels alive and vivid to them. And even without mania, much of art's energy is sexual. Or, as the quotation attributed to Renoir succinctly put it, "I paint with my penis." One rarely hears women exclaiming anatomical equivalencies, but there's little doubt that the silence does not negate the sensation. Aroused sexuality may stimulate creativity, intellectual and creative excitement may expand into seductive excitement, and both may boil over in messy ways. Furthermore, highly energetic, ambitious artists may possess large egos and large sexual appetites that want feeding.

People are sexual, so why focus on artists? Not because they are more sexual than other people. But because it would appear that sexuality gets engaged and named in particular ways around their work. More broadly, the nineteenth- and twentieth-century Anglo/European truism was that artists had to separate themselves from bourgeois society. They sometimes had to deny family expectation: Henri Matisse's decision, so disappointing to his father, to paint instead of practicing law; Charles Baudelaire's rebellion against his stepfather; Robert Louis Stevenson's refusal to become an engineer; Wordsworth's shirking of his familial assignment to join the church, to name a few examples. (A contemporary instance is described in Vietnamese-Australian writer Nam Le's short story "Love and Honor and Pity and Pride and Compassion and Sacrifice," in which a protagonist named Nam has seemingly defied his father's fierce insistence that he practice law and instead devotes himself to writing stories.) And, whether experiencing family support or not, the space in which these artists made art was often portrayed as a space of resistance. To see clearly, you had to stand back from the crowd.

So once they determined to shake off conventional expectations and place themselves outside of the common "life path" with work, why not with marriage and/or sex, too? Some of their choices may have been based in necessity: Without steady employ, a young male artist was deemed a poor prospect. And female art-makers who attempted to go public, however rare, seemed to have been confused in the collective mind with courtesans or other women of the night. (The decadent, prostitute-loving poet Baudelaire castigated his contemporary, the female novelist George Sand, as a "janitress," "kept woman," and "slut.")[15]

But why accept an identity of being someone without something when you could define yourself as possessing a variety of wealth that, in the form of freedom from convention, the bourgeoisie lacked? Whether true or not, the popular generalization that held, and may still quietly hold for some, was that artists construed the artist's life as superior for being freed of petty conventions, less materially focused, and sometimes guided by more flexible sexual mores. As Edna St. Vincent Millay's husband, Eugen Jan Boissevain, disdainfully summed up the fidelity of the more staid "other," "A completely faithful marriage is like an icebox with always some cold chicken in it."[16] He and Millay had a very open marriage. Millay famously claimed the worth of burning one's candle at both ends; meanwhile, her sonnets gorgeously recounted the aching losses that ensued.

Opposite truths coexist; generalizations are always iffy: There are as many ways to live as there are artists, and plenty live mundane, predictable lives and make fine art. I suspect a portion of the conceit of artists who believe their lives are noticeably different from most people's is a combination of vanity and ignorance. The vanity is an expression of a wish to support the strenuous efforts of art-making by feeling special. The ignorance is of the complexity of most people's lives. (It's hard to tease apart what behaviors are more shared than not, and which might particularly flow from talent or ambition, from achievement or fame.)

At the same time, something about the kinds of sacrifices art-making entails, and the way serious artists often really do have to place themselves apart from the larger group in order to say something (whether in words or otherwise) with more accuracy than is typically permitted in social discourse, may lead them to live lives that cluster around a different set of conventions. Perhaps, too, the awareness of their own creative energy, their sense of needing to express themselves through art, makes them feel different from early on. And possessing talent may itself be destabilizing, especially when accompanied by emotional conflict pressing for creative outlet.

So where does sexuality come into it? Obviously, everywhere. But particularly in some places. In his usual ironic, convoluted, and sneakily true way, Proust opined that writers choose sexual liaisons as a way both to improve their work and to detach themselves from other social pleasures they are compelled to give up in order to make space for their work. Speaking about the fictional novelist Bergotte, Proust's narrator M observes:

> *He knew that he could never produce such good work as in an atmosphere of amorous feelings. Love is too strong a word, but pleasure that is at all rooted in the flesh is helpful to literary work because it cancels all other pleasures, for instance the pleasures of society, those which are the same for everyone. And even if this love leads to disillusionment, it does at least stir, even by so doing, the surface of the soul which otherwise would be in danger of becoming stagnant.*[17]

PROUST SAYS, FIRST, that an atmosphere of amorous feelings produces good work; second, that sexual desire is a way for an artist to detach himself from his fellow men and therefore from feeling that he ought to conform to their standards. We don't know here exactly to which standards he refers, but we might guess that he means any that push artists to play the social game more than observe it, or that detract from their ability to see— to position themselves, really—in the between space (between desire and loss, past and future, real and unreal) they need to occupy in order to make art. And, as we've noted elsewhere, amorous feelings allow the artist to separate from his surroundings because the feelings keep him company and make him feel less alone.

His third claim is that sexual desire and liaisons enliven artists. It's not difficult to grasp what he means by the soul-stirring nature of eroticism and fresh love. Of equal interest are his words "stagnant" and "disillusionment." Proust implies here that you draw energy from the cycle of desire and disillusionment (a form of loss) in order to help you stay in the fantasy "between" so useful for art-making, and you choose this cycle in order to avoid stagnation. Whether the sexuality is the overt serial seductions that Proust assigns to Bergotte or the mostly more sublimated feelings that Lowell holds for Bishop, the different styles both are used psychologically to support the creative space.

But the larger notion to which Proust alludes, and which I keep trying to capture, is the psychological connection between creativity and eroticism, and what I would call "severed intimacy" (borrowing here a term Alfred Habegger uses in a different context in his biography of Emily Dickinson).[18] Often great creative energy seems either to be generated by, or at least to feed on, cycles wherein intimacy is psychologically or actually severed and then refound. One partial, mundane explanation for this phenomenon is that artists often disappear emotionally into their work and then, eventually, emerge, so the oscillation is dependent on a simple need for absence and then reconnection upon return. But likely this literal pattern is minor. Rather, I'm trying to capture something larger and less concrete.

An archetypal illustration of severed intimacy is Orpheus's trip to the underworld to win back Eurydice. As Bulfinch recounts the mythic tale, Orpheus, son of Apollo and the muse Calliope, is a musician who plays the lyre exquisitely. He marries Eurydice. But the young lovers are prematurely separated when Eurydice, fleeing a shepherd's advances, steps on a serpent and dies. Orpheus, bereft and desperate to see her again, travels to the underworld. There, accompanying his story with a melody from his lyre, he begs Hades and Persephone for the return of his bride. The beauty of his music is so extraordinary, so haunting, that the underworld comes to a standstill. As Bulfinch tells it, Sisyphus sits on his rock; the eagle pausing before the splayed Prometheus.[19]

Using the lyre to voice his desolation, Orpheus successfully pleads his case: The premature death has been too harsh to bear. Hades agrees to return Eurydice to life and to Orpheus. Eurydice will follow him as he climbs back into the world of the living. However, Hades admonishes, Orpheus must obey a single injunction: He must not glance back at her. If he does, she will die and be lost to him forever. Orpheus sets forth resolutely but, of course, he fails. He cannot resist the fierce pull to know if she is really as she was. His need to look, to reestablish contact with his beloved, is as overwhelming to him as his music had been to the underworld. The artist's urgency is to restore what has been severed.

But would that it were so straightforward. The tale represents a more complex psychological template: The other is lost to us; we go in search. We are filled with longing, with desire, with a willingness to do anything to win back the loving gaze— the source of psychological life and light. Our art-making is the embodiment of that profound distress, and, at the same time, it is the vehicle of our plea. And while this urgency to reconnect is emphasized, one cannot overlook the centrality of the unstated "minor chord," the disillusionment to which Proust refers, often accompanied by anger at abandonment—the knowledge that time has passed, and the original and particular opportunity offered by the lost other person can never be refound or fully recreated. One turns back at once to reassure oneself that the other is following—and yet, also, to send her away before she proves that the past is truly, irrevocably past.

Perhaps the artist's core psychological question is, Maybe fantasy—dreaming about you, longing for you in your absence, and transforming you into the symbolic representation of art—is ultimately the more bearable way to live in the world? That question, to some degree, belongs to every person. Artists may just have it bad. Or maybe artists are people who are hyperaware of this human circumstance and eager to capture it and represent it for all to share.

Loss and the severing of intimacy are human givens. At times, nothing is more relieving than to be free of the "other." But often, nothing is more crucial to the psyche than the moments of waiting for return. For a child, that return is life-and-death, and the adult artist, though he departs so as to create space to work, retains and expresses the child's dire question through his art. The threat of psychological death and the concomitant longing contribute to the impetus for heightened creativity. You learn to finger your lyre exquisitely as a way to woo the gods who will decide your fate.

Perhaps for people who become artists there's something sharply traumatic about the particular experience of loss: Eurydice is taken from Orpheus suddenly, prematurely, while their love is young. The severing itself is ruthless. And the pain and grief that ensue may provoke the creative expression initially as an effort to make sense of the absurd horror, or to take control of one's aloneness, as an effort of undoing, to provide balm, or to woo the other to return.

In this sense, the creative impulse is like the oyster's pearl-making, where the severed intimacy functions as an irritant of sand. The creativity flows forth first as a response to the stress created by the wound, then by the release of the imaginative restitution—of restoring the lost love. Eroticism gets stirred up in part because one is excited by the upsurge of energy in the fantasies, and because sexuality naturally joins the reconnecting urgency. The imaginative act is an undoing of the unbearable loss and a restoration of one's sense of personal power together with the anticipated strength that will result from the reconnection. It restores, as well, the fantasy of another person who will deeply—almost magically—appreciate us and our productions. The identity of artist becomes a way of naming and validating the wish to produce something unequivocally worthy of that appreciation.

Whether or not you resonate with this psychological template, the larger point is that each person who stays with artmaking needs to create an emotional space where the creative work can occur, which is psychologically neither too close nor too far away from others. And during that time, you must find a way not just continually to rebalance privacy and solitude and intimacy as needed, but also to maintain your own sense of the value of your effort and to maintain your identity as an artist—which in turn grants you more authority with which to keep working. Using mostly letters, Lowell and Bishop offered this great gift to each other.

They intuitively understood that letters allowed the everyday mess of their own feelings to be contained in a fashion that did not sever them from each other. Or let me put it another way:

Almost paradoxically, the fact of a letter, itself an object holding feelings severed from a person and a moment, traveling to a destination, seemed to protect them from severing the friendship. They achieved this constancy in part, too, by keeping too much disruptive in-person contact at bay.

The last letter in the correspondence, many years later, is Bishop's to Lowell on August 2, 1977. She is ill but will live two more years. He will die suddenly six weeks later. It begins on a note that makes the final statement of their motif: "Dear Cal: I'm writing to you & to Mary [McCarthy] this morning to say that I hope you'll understand if I say I'd rather you don't come to North Haven on the 10th or whenever."[20] Don't come near. Don't look firsthand on my wreck of a life. Don't risk diminishing your belief in my poetry, your regard for me as a poet. Stay away. Write me a letter about our shared labor.

CHAPTER 7

ruthlessness

I

I N AN ESSAY some years ago I briefly raised the question of ruthlessness and art-making. Since then, the subject has lingered in the back of my mind. Like so many nascent ideas, this one has felt warm to the touch but without explicit features. What do I mean by "ruthlessness"? Do great artists possess more than their share of what we might describe as the overt or tacit willingness to disregard, or walk over, or hurt others either to create a masterwork or in pursuit of success? Do you have to possess some to make art well? Will its absence impede your forward motion? Hoping to clarify my thinking, I read Patrick O'Brian's biography of Pablo Picasso. Before I had paged halfway through its considerable bulk, I realized that O'Brian was so identified with his subject he protectively omitted details that could have shed light on my inquiry. When you are as great a genius as Picasso, O'Brian's silence suggests, any ruthlessness that exists is irrelevant, because its damage is trivial beside the oeuvre. In the back of my mind, I remember reading in a review of Arianna Huffington's biography of Picasso that the painter had a world-class cruel streak, but I also remember reviewers criticizing as overwrought her take on his misogyny, unkindness, and familial neglect.

"Ruthless" according *to Merriam-Webster's* is "having no ruth: merciless, cruel." "Ruth," a word I cannot remember ever hearing in daily parlance, is "compassion for the misery of another" and "sorrow for one's own faults: remorse." "Remorse," in turn, is glossed as "a gnawing distress arising from a sense of guilt for past wrongs: self-reproach." So, to be ruthless is to be merciless, to lack compassion and remorse: to lack serious distress or guilt about one's own merciless behaviors.

Ruthlessness has two major domains of meaning when it comes to art-making, and the mercilessness of the artist is different depending on which one we consider. The first concerns the artist's life; the second, his or her art. I'm not certain there's a clean separation between the two, but they are not interchangeable either.

Let me begin by circling back to my long-ago example. One late summer day, I had given my father a three-page short story to read in which a man decides against killing a pig because his

son loves the creature and finds the notion of slaughtering it unbearable. A colleague had clipped the brief fiction from a magazine, and he and I had used it in a summer course for adolescents.
I had found it moving. My father, on the other hand, felt the
writing was mediocre. To make his point, he showed me a par-
allel moment in *Jude the Obscure* by Thomas Hardy, a writer
whom he greatly admired. That scene displays Jude's difficulty
killing an animal and foreshadows the protagonist's failure to
live his life well.

Jude and his wife, Arabella, cannot afford to hire a butcher,
so they must slaughter their pig themselves. Arabella knows they
will earn more money if the meat has been "well bled"—and
insists that the pig must die slowly to bleed clean. Jude cannot
stand to make the animal suffer, and he finds the task of killing
it dreadful:

> *"Upon my soul I would sooner have gone without the*
> *pig than have had this to do!" said Jude. "A creature I*
> *have fed with my own hands."*
>
> *[Arabella implores him:] "Don't be such a tender-*
> *hearted fool! There's the sticking-knife—the one with*
> *the point. Now whatever you do, don't stick un too*
> *deep." . . .*
>
> *"The meat must be well bled, and to do that he must*
> *die slow. We shall lose a shilling a score if the meat is red*
> *and bloody! Just touch the vein, that's all. I was brought*

up to it, and I know . . . He ought to be eight or ten min-
utes dying, at least." . . .

[Jude dismisses her knowledge and refuses:] "He shall
not be half a minute if I can help it, however the meat
may look," said Jude determinedly.[1]

JUDE STABS THE pig hard, and kills it quickly, sparing the beast
at the couple's expense, and simultaneously demonstrating to
Arabella that he is not tough or comprehending enough to act in
their world in ways that might let him live up to his aspirations or
help the couple and their children prosper. To put it another way,
Jude is too filled with ruth. He has too much empathy for the
animal, too much compassion for its misery, to act as effectively
on his own behalf as his survival demands.

How much ruth versus ruthlessness to bring to bear in life
is everybody's problem, though it is often finessed and rarely
frankly named. (Most people like to think of themselves as virtuous, a concept that breaks out in hives when self-awareness
of ruthlessness comes around.) Determining appropriate aggression, and syncing it with justice, love, and remorse, constitutes
the ur-quandary behind millennia of religious and moral pon-
dering. Each context defines, often tacitly, how much self-assertion cum aggression is acceptable, even favored, and how much
makes someone an outlier—either through Jude-like empathy
and timidity or, conversely, through excessive hardheartedness
and love of smiting. Do you kill the pig too quickly or too slowly,

too reluctantly, too readily, or not at all? And what implications does your decision have for your particular life, and for your kin?

It is no accident that Hardy put Jude in the pig-killing predicament. Not only was the novelist conveying the severity of his characters' circumstance, but I suspect he was aware of how intimate the question is to art. Artists—especially dedicated or ambitious ones—have to deal continually with their own ruthlessness. Their actions cannot be handed off; one cannot simply decide to pay a slaughterhouse and look away.

Art-making (and here is one of the places it separates from simpler forms of craft) requires great courage. Sometimes it is the courage to keep going in the face of doubt and psychological conundrum; sometimes it is to "say" what many may not want to hear. Or it can be the courage to show frankly what is before you, to defy current convention, to push the limits of a form, to risk foolishness, to challenge the past, or simply to reveal bald difference. And, perhaps most of all, it requires courage because failure is assured. Even the greatest, most fully realized artists can see beyond their work, to what their work might have been.

Courage and ruthlessness are not the same, but they can overlap. Ruthlessness can be a by-product of the artist's courage, or it can be gratuitous, or it can be what is eschewed—a marker of the place where courage gave way. The painter Mary Cassatt commented about John Singer Sargent that "He cared too much what other people thought."[2] Cassatt apparently felt that Sargent lacked adequate courage to offend—a kind of failure of ruthlessness; she implied that the quality of his work was hobbled by his wish to please.

Even the honing of one's ability to comprehend art sometimes requires the severing of easy loves, of sentimental inclinations or too much ruth, as my father attempted to demonstrate to me with Thomas Hardy. I was twenty-one and wanted him to share my excitement as I finished my first teaching job. He wanted me to feel the difference between a top-drawer writer and someone in a lower tier. He sought to initiate me, to teach me a standard he held dear.

I have held our pig exchange variously at different times, though in the moment I experienced it as unnecessarily harsh, even, in its own way, a little ruthless. A truth that lingers now is how much the ruthlessness dilemma haunted his own life, and how deeply and personally he felt the moment in Hardy's novel that he read aloud to me. My father was an artist who possessed great compassion and great ambition. He understood Jude's feelings, and he understood Arabella's. He announced his intention to become a successful writer at fifteen, not long after his mother died or committed suicide in a mental asylum. He worked at it relentlessly, spending almost two decades seriously poor, practicing and refining his skill before he began publishing stories. Once he married, he felt responsible to support his family and so he taught full-time as well as wrote. Furthermore, he wanted to be a good family man, at least in his fashion, and a loving father.

The resulting emotional conflict of where and how to spend his hours tested him sorely, particularly because, in order to achieve the quality to which he aspired, he had to put his writing first much of the time. And this priority created a predicament: How do you balance sacrifices? When do you give in to your wife's admonitions and your children's pleadings and join them for a Sunday at the beach? When do you abandon them again in order to spend the day in your office reworking a page of prose? How much time do you give to your students, or to colleagues and friends who ask for your help with their work? (Elena Delbanco, daughter of the great cellist Bernard Greenhouse, described on NPR how she used to erase the names of his cello students scheduled for a given day, and write in her own name, hoping, futilely, that he might grant her one of their hours.)[3]

So, too, when do you diminish further your scant family time, departing the marriage secretly to pursue liaisons, because fresh seduction and romance fuel your ego and your work? And where the work itself is concerned, how often do you describe friends and intimates in overly frank ways in your fiction, come what may? Or, conversely, when do you leave a great story untold to protect someone you love? (I lately heard a writer describe how he had stopped working on a memoir about his dead parents because he found it unbearable to portray them to the world in the fashion that was emerging in his text.) And, how much of your own short life do you give over to the book-lined room with the desk where you sit, pen in hand?

Most artists and non-artists alike have pondered variants of these questions, yet we tend to think of ruthlessness when we picture financiers or commandos, not people sketching with pastels or composing music. While the artist's ruthlessness may be cosmically of a miniscule order beside the despot's, it is of interest because of the way conflict about one's own aggression—or even one's healthy entitlement—inhibits or facilitates the creative process, contributes to defining the quality of the work, and promotes or hinders the realizing of ambition. It is also of interest because we traditionally associate artists with beauty and mystery, and we are uneasy noting the harm that can be a by-product of creativity.

In her memoir *Night Studio* about her father, the painter Philip Guston, Musa Mayer describes behavior by both her parents that in the context of this discussion passes muster as ruthless, at least with a small "r," and that sheds light on the meanings of the term. Guston was born in 1913 in Montreal, the fifth of seven children in a very poor family only recently immigrated from Russia.[4] They moved to Los Angeles where Guston's father, Leib, scraped by for a while as a junkman, gathering up and reselling rags and other discards. Leib became depressed, and his despair gradually overwhelmed him. Philip was either ten or eleven when he came home and found his father dead, hanging from a rafter. The traumatized boy started drawing seriously the following year and worked at it assiduously in spite of difficult circumstances, including his favorite brother's sudden death while they were both still teenagers.

By the time Philip was married and a father, he had strung a thick curtain between his adult life and what had come before—at least as far as talking about it. And his daughter grew up ignorant of his past. She rarely met any of her kin and knew none of them well. After he died in 1980, she set about filling in gaps, looking up relatives, and trying to make sense of her own childhood. As she learned about Guston's early life, she understood for the first time its frequent representation in his paintings and the way objects that had seemed randomly chosen actually carried personal history. Her discoveries heighten the reader's sense, and no doubt her own, of how sorely anguish and memory dogged him.

Knowing even a little about Guston's life, it's also easy to grasp how the single-mindedness of his focus on his art is simultaneously the single-mindedness a desperate man must possess to climb a rope up through flames and exit a burning pit. However loosely and broadly we apply the term "creativity," nowhere does it gather more transcendent meaning than in this use: when artists wrestle with the large emotions created by what has happened to them and transform them into something that happens for all of us. Orchestrating the transformation strains all muscles.

The father Mayer portrays in her memoir is a compelling, talented, traumatized and traumatizing, serious person, and a profoundly selfish one. He lives for his painting. Signed on to the mission, his wife always puts him first in their family life, where he also places himself—sometimes to a dumbfounding extent. (His daughter writes, "My father's needs always came

first. I never thought to question this; it was axiomatic; an article of faith.")[5] During a time when the family was terribly poor,
and food short, if his wife (also named Musa, so I'll refer to the
daughter by her nickname, Ingie) offered an extra bit of bread
to their growing child instead of to him, Philip would object and
complain, experiencing his daughter as a depriving rival rather
than as offspring to be nurtured. Musa also gave up her own
painting to better support his, and the memoir recounts a home
life that had little room for compromise in the allocation of re-
sources or for competition or support between equal adults.

After her father's death, researching for her book, Ingie
asked Musa how Philip had felt about their having children: "My
mother paused for what seemed like a long time before answering. 'He didn't want children,' she finally said. 'His work, well—
you know. It was everything.'" Musa then recalls that when she
became pregnant, "'Philip was terribly upset. He was simply beside himself, saying I had ruined his life. I thought I had done
something quite dreadful.'" Ingie notes, "My mother stopped and
looked at me as if suddenly concerned that what she was revealing might disturb me, then went on hurriedly to say, 'Of course,
when you arrived it was entirely different. Once he saw you.'"[6]

In 1948, having won a Prix de Rome, Guston left his family
for a year so he could live in Italy and look at art and perhaps
break through an impasse that had developed in his painting.
Neither his wife nor his daughter fared well while he was away.
The next summer, the mother departed for four months to join

her husband, leaving the six-year-old on her own in a series of difficult camp experiences. When the parents returned, they noticed that the child's personality had been transformed from curious and lively to shy and subdued.[7]

> *"I shouldn't have left you," my mother tells me now, "but when Philip wrote and asked me to come, I didn't think of you. I thought only of being with him, that he wanted me with him."*
>
> *"Couldn't you have taken me with you?" I ask.*
>
> *My mother looks at me, aghast. "Taken you? Oh, I wouldn't have known how. Philip didn't want you there."*

CAREENING IN THE wake of her mother's bluntness, the daughter suggests it was terrible for him to make her mother choose between them. The elder Musa responds, "Terrible? But why? He was an *artist*. That was simply who he was."[8]

Putting aside for a moment sentiments that could variously be called ruthless maternal honesty and/or dismal parenting, part of what makes the exchange relevant is Musa's unequivocal idea of an artist. Artist with a capital "A." These days we mostly hear such claims in parodies, but I certainly remember when they were made unironically—at least in our household and some of the communities in which I grew up. (Most notably, the one filled with artists. John Logan's play *Red*, about the painter Mark Rothko, vividly evokes that era and perspective.) The notion, as Musa expounds it, is that the artist doesn't play by everyman's rules. So, if you marry one, you know that you will put him first, and that you will not receive from him the husbanding that other women might expect because his calling demands that he put his art first, before any one intimate relationship.

And while it's easy to feel wearied by the entitlement of the claim, there's truth in it, too. The most serious and dedicated art-making encourages artists to put a huge amount of themselves into their work—an enterprise that may be separate from their additional need to support their families financially and raise children. Even after hours, when she is no longer casting bronzes, a sculptor is often seeking out peers to help her keep up on the current art scene, compare notes, and inspire herself. Likewise, on many evenings, writers are reading, composers attending concerts, photographers gallery hopping, dramatists viewing plays, and so on. To realize significant work, a serious artist will certainly feel tempted to trade away, sacrifice, or ignore a good chunk of the everyday dimensions of family life. Sometimes this eschewing is intrinsic to the demands of the work (and likely no more prevalent than with driven professionals, politicians, or businesspeople or with people who have to work two and three jobs at minimum wage just to pay the bills); other times there may be a destructive, inflated self-importance that blends with necessity. (My muse will be unhappy if I have to wash the dishes or put the kids to bed. Sue Halpern captures this kind of posturing perfectly in her review of Walter Isaacson's biography of Steve Jobs. She writes,

[Jobs] was a bully, a dissembler, a cheapskate, a dead-beat dad, a manipulator, and sometimes he was very nice. Isaacson does not shy away from any of this, and the trouble is that Jobs comes across as such a repellent man, cruel even to his best friend Steve Wozniak, derisive of almost everyone, ruthless to people who thought they were his friends, indifferent to his daughters, that the book is often hard to read . . . Jobs himself dismissed his excesses with a single word: artist. Artists, he seemed to believe, got a pass on bad behavior. [9]

WE COLLECTIVELY SEEM uncertain about how much bad behavior is the real underbelly of genius, how much a self-indulgence.)

MUSA'S MARITAL GRATIFICATION arrived indirectly, like something hidden or smuggled. Her satisfaction came from creating the conditions that furthered her husband's work; her mutuality from being in the presence of a creative person, which offered the opportunity of witnessing his art-making and art up close, and from the honoring request, sometimes, to express opinions as well as admire. They also shared private intimacies unknown to their child or anyone else. Yet it was not easy. And in time, the wife's sense of being loved became so agile, so adept at gleaning sparse fields, she managed to find sustenance even in her husband's returning to her after his dalliances.

This supporting role plus the paintings were the marital gifts Guston had to give. And when he was especially exhilarated about a work in progress, and often quite drunk, he sometimes woke Musa in the middle of the night to have her look upon it with him. Eventually, when he became successful, she shared the money he earned and felt the satisfaction, pride, and reflected glory of his openings, his followers, and his acclaim.

Meanwhile, Musa's belief, or theirs, creates more of a predicament for Ingie, who, like all children, is born into the family enterprise without opportunity to grant informed consent about either its aims or its emotional costs. You get a sense that she is often an afterthought. Yet Guston's gifts to his daughter include upward mobility, likely some inherited wealth, and a father who, however preoccupied and absent, did not kill himself. He demonstrated to her how a person saves his own life, and how an artist fills a bare canvas. There's little doubt he gave her, emotionally and materially, more than he had been given. Yet her reality commences with her own entry into the world, and she often experienced his behavior as destructive, even devastating; although less visible, the psychological body blows she absorbed are as real as his paint. Cut off from his past, his thrashing about must have appeared to her as shadowboxing that punched real bystanders. In a sense, what reads here as parental ruthlessness can also be seen as the collateral damage of an intense, all-consuming fight between a man and himself as he struggles to assimilate his own past (as well as the great painters who preceded him) and to produce original work.

Musa Guston is hardly the only person to feel reverence for artists. And it's interesting to ask why exactly many are so inclined (beyond the fact that we seem hardwired to feel reverence now and then). Yes, because they can make art, and so embody the mystery of how some people manage remarkable or even exquisite things while the rest of us fumble. Artists divert us and entertain us, thrill us and disgust us, enlighten us and baffle us, and they offer companionship. If we think of art as a bucket holding within it our whole invisible feeling life, they are the bold "guys" who dip their hands in and fetch out the gorgeous and the gross for the rest of us to see. They offer us back to ourselves wet, fresh, and thrashing.

Artists also represent a relatively peaceable version of the collective, oft-felt wish to defy our puniness and leave a mark on the indifferent world around us. Some years ago I descended into a cave in the Dordogne in France, to look at a 20,000- or 30,000-year-old handprint carefully painted onto a dank, rough wall. The cave painter had filled a reed with a powdery red pigment, then blown the color over his hand, leaving an imprint for the ages and an ur-painting. While it was a much simpler image than the extraordinary tableaus of animals in Lascaux, or Chauvet-Pont-d'Arc, seeing it up close raised the hairs on the back of my neck.

We tend to make artists special not just because they will scrunch for days in odd positions in order to inscribe the musculature of a horse upon a rock surface deep underground, but also because we ask their works to map the outer edge of what is psychologically, aesthetically, technically, and imaginatively possible. We ask them to move us deeply. To appropriate Kafka's famous thought about books, we ask their works to labor as ice axes breaking "the frozen sea within us."

And one way we sometimes attempt to reconcile our species' temperamental contradictions is to conflate artists with their work. We superimpose our awe at the cave paintings onto the artists who painted them. Or we assume that if someone carves a Pietà, he must be saintly. We say that he or she is a great artist, and from there it is an easy mental elision to make him or her a great human being. Even though we know better, we can still feel ever so slightly queasy fully loving a beautiful object or verse whose very creation communed somehow with harm. (One good example of this phenomenon was the post–World War II generation's ambivalence about attending performances of operas by the rabidly anti-Semitic composer Richard Wagner.)

No doubt this curiosity about the connection between art and maker also contributes to our fascination with artists as rogues. Caravaggio comes to mind. His brutality opposes the care and detail we find in his work and confounds our wish for consistency. In recent decades, we have—living a contradiction without reconciling it—tended to romanticize some artists exactly because they are unsteady, and we've admired their art as the gold salvaged from their shipwrecked lives (Jackson Pollock, Mark Rothko, Sylvia Plath, David Foster Wallace, and on and on). We idealized them oppositely. Not for any simple human greatness or proximity to the gods, but for their art's intimacy with such visible suffering. Readers of their biographies, and the media generally, seem to be fascinated, too, by their impact on intimates. (When, for example, the forty-seven-year-old Nicholas Hughes, an ecologist working in Alaska and son of Sylvia Plath, committed suicide in 2009, forty-six years after Plath's suicide, there was plenty of media attention including an op-ed in *The New York Times*.)

And whereas we might want art-makers to be less than harmful, some claim otherwise. The poet W. H. Auden opined, "Real artists are not nice people. All their best feelings go into their work and life has the residue." In her short biography of James Joyce, the novelist Edna O'Brien asked rhetorically,

> *Do writers have to be such monsters in order to create? I believe that they do. It is a paradox that while wrestling with language to capture the human condition they become more callous, and cut off from the very human traits which they so glisteningly depict. There can be no outer responsibility, no interruptions; only the ongoing inner drone, rhythmic, insistent, struggling to make a living moment of both beauty and austerity.*[10]

ONE INTERESTING WAY to hold all these contradictory perceptions struck me when, as I was revising this chapter, I found that others before me had also noted the large link between accomplishment and early parental death. According to one argument, early parental death creates a profound loss of safety, which energizes and focuses some resilient children or adolescents on excelling as a way to enhance safety. (As I noted earlier, I believe that the psychological loss of the parent can have a similar impact, even if no one has actually died. Marcel Proust is one example.)[11]

For our purposes, we could suggest that sometimes the artist's sense of safety moves from being found in human intimacy to being primarily located in her labor to master an art form and/or create a satisfying imaginative world for herself—both of which she can control. The notion fits well with a number of people we've discussed in this book—Keats, Wordsworth, Guston, Lowell, Bishop, Chaplin. And it reiterates more broadly what we have already suggested about Guston: One way to understand the artist's ruthlessness is as a by-product of his singular survival focus.

Obvious, but worth repeating, is that plenty of fine artists had loving parents or intact families. Their ambition is piqued for other reasons. What ruthlessness they possess has other sources.

II

But what about the rest of us? What if we have not lost parents, and/or we are not as focused as Philip Guston, or geniuses like Picasso or Joyce, and are perhaps just trying to master a craft or make art more modestly? Why do we have to contend with the question of ruthlessness?

First of all, because time is ruthless. It consumes us indifferently. Each art-maker's or craftsman's one, only, unrepeatable life is the stack slapped down on the table whenever the croupier spins the wheel. The terms are stark; nothing is guaranteed; and if a person cares only about the realm of significant accomplishments, he or she may give everything and get little back. What if all Guston's efforts had been in vain, and he'd never shown a painting, or if he'd sat in his studio for years and never painted one? The creation of significant work, much less a masterpiece or great oeuvre, the garnering of financial success or fame, is rare. Ruthlessness comes into play because so many wager so much, and make diverse sacrifices without winning the pile of chips. A photographer can spend decades taking pictures and never find a gallery to represent her, or even a single buyer. That reality can be devastating or less consequent depending on how she's framed her purpose. I once heard the writer Richard Bausch note that literature is like music. We read a great play or book not to get to the end, but to enjoy each note of the song. People making art who possess a portion of that feeling toward their own labor are more likely to harvest the joy of the enterprise separate from the achievement. Still, most of us also need some fantasy of audience and success to sharpen our effort and push us along through its difficulties; so a balance can be hard to find even as it is crucial to seek.

Meanwhile, mastering a craft and practicing it, especially if you are simultaneously holding a day job or looking after children and a household, are no simple matter of nine to five. The hours are stolen. Even when aims are relatively modest, all art-makers and craftsmen have to decide how much of themselves—their time, their emotional and physical energy, their money, their lost wages—to put into their work.

How much support can you expect from those around you? Is it fair to ask your mate to earn disproportionately to pick up the slack created by your underpaid effort? Is it fair to hire extra sitters or lean on the grandparents and sometimes see less of your spouse or kids so you can make your way to your studio after hours? What can you scrape together out of the family budget to buy the musical instrument you need or to pay for lessons? (The most striking revelation in Renée Fleming's memoir about her life as an opera diva is of the endless lessons, not simply of voice and performance, but of movement, foreign language, elocution, and on and on.) Is it good for your family if you work in your studio all day of the two weeks you're on vacation? What if you leave them to spend a year in Rome alone because there's a good chance the experience will help you improve your work, but there's only one travel stipend? When does your self-absorption start causing harm you cannot either accept or rationalize away?

At the same time, if you are too well endowed with "ruth" and you don't grasp that it is inevitable that you must face these vexing questions, that to bring a work into the world you must sometimes act from parts of yourself that cannot by any stretch of the imagination be called attractive, that too much "nice" is a death-kiss for adequate audacity, serious effort, or originality, then you may give up on your work without consciously calling it quits. You are likely to retreat from the difficult decisions. And you will end up feeling that you have failed at something you sought—rather than knowing you consciously weighed its price to you, at this moment in your life, and chose to pursue it or not. Though decent people must continually attempt to curtail their elbows, adults who hurt no one are either living like beetles trapped in glass bottles, or in danger of becoming everyone else's mark, or self-deluded, or unusually lucky, or saints. And while some may be ruthless, and/or blind to their own behaviors, the rest of us who can—at least sometimes—see how we transgress can only attempt to make amends and to live with our remorse. Still, accepting the real terms of this conundrum permits a somewhat more enlightened stance in anything you do, including the work of mastery.

In truth, the most ruthless gesture many of us might need to learn is the simple but uncomfortable one of saying "No," both to others and to the parts of ourselves that feel too guilty or embarrassed if we do not always put family, friends, and other obligations first before our work. "No, I cannot get together today for coffee; no, I won't chaperone the class outing this time; no, I'm afraid you'll have to go without me to visit your sister; no, I'm really sorry, but I won't be able to watch your hockey game this week." The dilemma is hardest where our children are concerned.

Even when artists and craftsmen earn for their labor, and have more flexible schedules than other workers outside the home, and are physically more present in their families, and are happier for possessing an absorbing errand, they may be psychologically preoccupied with their work in progress. When the distractedness is low-key, it's nothing. When it's intense, it can alter the landscape and feel depriving to intimates.

Years ago, I spent many hours with a friend who is now a successful pianist, and in time I realized that the two of us were conducting the friendship in different dialects. His mind was in his music, as were many of his emotions. Many evenings, I'd sit beside him at the piano, and he'd play whatever he was practicing as well as any and every piece I wished to hear. I felt as nurtured as one does by a friend who listens well. And I have rarely heard music with such pleasure or acuity since. But had he been a romantic partner, I would have found his preoccupation depriving.

On the other hand, there are legions of people besides Musa—Tom Levine, the brother of the fabulously overextended conductor James Levine, is one contemporary example; Vladimir Nabokov's wife, Vera, another famous one; Horst Kettner, Leni Riefenstahl's much, much younger lover and deathbed husband; all the women who surrounded Wordsworth (and made Coleridge gnaw his hands in envy); to name a few among many—who clearly find ongoing satisfaction in caring for their very busy and preoccupied creative kin and smoothing the way for them each day.

III

WHEN THE INTENSE desire for fame dominates over the wish to create, ruthlessness takes a different turn. Great ambition for public recognition often requires its own extreme single-mindedness. Yet in the process, the preeminence of art-making can become displaced or corrupted. The fierce hunger for adulation is like a Trojan horse that sometimes sneaks imposters through art's gates.

In some ways, Leni Riefenstahl is a poor choice for a discussion of ruthlessness because she spent so many post–World War II years as the poster child of awful artist behavior. On the other hand, it's remarkable she wasn't put to death after the war when so many lesser collaborators were executed.

As a young woman, Riefenstahl tied her wagon, or perhaps her lingerie, to Hitler's rising star, and she spent the Nazi years wined and dined as the regime's darling. During the war, when almost every serious artist in Germany was murdered, forced into exile, or jailed, she prospered and became world famous. She lived lavishly in a big house (which some say Hitler bought for her) with a fancy car and was able to dress to the nines, travel where she wished, spend what she wanted, and party on the A-list of the most elite Nazi social events. She was the consummate insider. No one but Hitler himself had say over her movie-making budgets, and since he both loved her films glorifying his regime and believed that hers was the true and sublime German sensibility, he rarely refused her entreaties for more cash. *Triumph of the Will* and *Olympia* (her film of the 1936 Olympics in Berlin) are classic works of crowd-stirring propaganda.

However repugnant her love affair with Nazism, observers tend to grant that Riefenstahl worked ferociously hard, and that she was guided by a strong aesthetic sense that made her into a serious innovator of film, both in movies and in photography. She had grit and physical courage. As a young woman during her early career in front of the camera, she was willing to ask anything of herself—climbing glaciers, hiking mountains barefoot—to make a scene work. She sustained injuries that would have retired reasonable people and kept going. Later, as a director, she repeatedly pushed herself so hard to perfect her official Reich film projects that she more than once collapsed in nervous exhaustion.

Riefenstahl appears to have been almost completely amoral. Her signature refrain was an insouciant, prescient, deeply revealing, and, in her context, appalling bon mot: "Reality doesn't interest me."[12] In 1939, assigned to film Hitler's armies as they marched into Poland, she witnessed an early civilian massacre by German soldiers. On this occasion she protested vehemently about the army's behavior both to a general and to Hitler himself. In that moment she seems to have felt overwhelmed by horror and by ruth. During the war she experienced a series of illnesses and nervous breakdowns, as well as periods of deep depression that suggest the moral contradiction within her choices did plague her however hard she tried to push conflict from her mind. But she generally accepted the terms of her success, turning a world-class blind eye to brutality and genocide in order to harvest cash and fame.

Riefenstahl's ruthlessness has broad scope and large consequence. She wildly glorified Nazi virtue and encouraged a nation to delude itself. If ever we could place responsibility for deaths and suffering on the doorstep of an artist (though some would feel she should simply be called a propagandist), Riefenstahl's movies make the case for her culpability. After the war many people despised her. She spent decades trying to cover her tracks and edit her story—first to spare her life, and then to allow her to reestablish a career. It's unclear whether she registered any true remorse or shame. Certainly, her public actions suggest not.

Rather, it seems she substituted charisma and vitality for conscience, and she published her last book of photography when she was 100 years old. She died at 101, still controversial, but widely honored and largely rehabilitated with few of her fans bothering to distinguish propaganda or image from art. And, in a sense, it was her genius for confusing the two domains that made her prescient and historically important.

To find a current celebrity who embodies the hunger for adulation as intently as Riefenstahl, we need look no further than

Lady Gaga—Stefani Germanotto. I know of no performer alive who seeks fame as ferociously (and ably) as she does. As she herself noted, "I will kill to get what I need." Yet, she disavows her ruthlessness even as she baldly states it. (In a voice-over in the *Marry the Night* video, uncannily reiterating Riefenstahl, Gaga proclaims, "It's not that I've been dishonest, it's just that I loathe reality." Later she adds, perhaps ironically or subversively, perhaps in a Steve Jobs grab for justification, "Mais je suis une artiste." But I am an artist.)[13]

While some would say Lady Gaga's music-making represents serious artistry, others would claim its chief purpose is display. Her videos are sometimes compelling and fresh, sometimes kitsch, slick, campy, often soft-porny, fast-paced, and strange; and they are advertisements. Germanotto is a brilliant advertiser—primarily of herself, her life, her costumes, her psyche, her sexual fantasies, and her body. But there's also plenty of product placement. Indeed, some of the videos can be viewed as vehicles to sell telephones, computers, or bottles of liquor. Her songs are energetic and catchy. Only time will tell how much her work will stand as a talented, self-aware send-up of commodity culture and extreme self-display, and how much it will wear thin, revealed as psychological need posturing as art. Clearly, it contains both, and the balance shimmers—and wobbles.

Still, Lady Gaga's combination of sexual trope, media savvy, creative energy, talent, and huge drive, together with the quick camera work of her pieces, keeps viewers entertained and fans enraptured. (Several of her videos on YouTube have more than 100 million views, and *Bad Romance* has been watched almost half a billion times, a dumbfounding number—and one that trounces Michael Jackson.) Her grandiose video struggles—for example, between good and evil in *Judas*—represent battles as old as time now conducted by Stefani's avatar on a new global media level. "Jesus," she sings, "is my virtue. Judas is the demon I cling to."[14]

You can read this fantasy struggle as correlative for her own turmoil as she tries to clamber up to the top of fame's pig pile and still preserve a sense of herself as a good person. (To the degree she possesses artistic ruthlessness, it appears to be located in the verisimilitude of some of her video enactments of her own psychic struggles.) Germanotto attended Catholic schools, so it's not hard to imagine the sources of her conflicted imagery. But its meaning to her is less clear. Watch her for a while, and you realize that the constant, kaleidoscopic camera cuts in her videos keep action from possessing consequence. Everything, including the results of her mock violence and sexual posing, disappears as fast as it appears. Inner and outer worlds merge. All is virtual. She'll do anything, but none of it matters—a view that reflects accurately something about the current zeitgeist, and likely also reflects our collective, larger confusions about what, if anything, remains real or consequent in our media-dominated and distorted, ever-more-virtual existence. At her best, Lady Gaga riffs on this contemporary absurdity. (Ironically, she also demonstrates the long-term impact of Riefenstahl's "innovations" as a propagandist, the way Riefenstahl's use of film documentary to create a false world purporting to be true has evolved across time into a huge cultural muddle about whether there can be any such thing as truth or even shared reality.)

When you explore the media coverage of Lady Gaga, you see how the more she becomes a megastar, the more she—or her handlers—at once exploits and yet carefully softens the over-the-top ambitious dimension of her drive. She seems intent on having her fans love her because she is a nice Catholic family girl who likes to cook, and is close to her parents, and who supports good causes and yet is equally intent on having them love her for how "bad" and "out there" and immodest she can be. The contradiction would be completely tenable if she didn't leave the impression that self-promotion is her uber-goal, and that her other efforts, claims, and self-portrayals just might be in its service.

In exchange for their adoration, she gives herself to her fans. As I was thinking about this phenomenon (and the ruthless toll it will likely take on what genuine personhood she possesses), I shuddered. What if one day she just wanted to be the old, anonymous, private Stephani again? It seems impossible. Even the witness protection program can't safely transform her back. She is possessed by her alter ego and its legion of followers. Will she be the rare person who can surf that wave? Or will she eventually tire and drown under it? Time will tell.

When interviewed on talk shows, Lady Gaga presents herself as a "freak" or outsider, who—she tells Ellen DeGeneres and the television audience—defines her music-making as a space where she can feel safe and unafraid and as a way to share that radical self-acceptance with her fans.[15] She describes a nervous breakdown, and displays her vulnerability, her sense of herself as an outcast, the "Mother Monster." She tells the audience on *The View*, "Getting picked on in school, it sticks with you for life."[16] She suggests that if she can be totally out there and still feel okay about herself, her fans can feel okay about themselves, too.

Lady Gaga has an antibullying foundation and publicly opposed "Don't ask, don't tell." (As one of my sons noted, she likely had more positive political impact by taking that position than most us can have in a lifetime.) When on *Oprah*, she counsels her audience to spend five minutes a day feeling compassionate feelings for themselves—as, she told them, she tried to do each day for herself.[17] Her decency seems sincere. But it lies uneasily with her madly ambitious claims. ("I'm going to be a fucking superstar," she exults on a trailer for a *60 Minutes* stint.)[18] *So,* she appears to be saying, *I have ruthless ambition, but I am not ruthless; I am a very good, very nice person—albeit with a dark side.* Perhaps she is right. Yet such a severing seems in part like a defiant fantasy or at least an impossible distance to bridge. At moments, she resembles a sexualized child dressing up and playing adult. And her success can partly be located in the way she embodies and mirrors back the great contemporary distress about how to grow up, and how to survive, when so much in the world is disrupted and nuts.

Still, Lady Gaga grasps (from her own great need, if not from conscious perception) that self-love is what mass culture is offering up (selling) as sustenance to people—as the oxygen tank in an otherwise airless landscape. And, unsupported by much else, it's paltry. Ruthlessness seems to get disavowed and deemed inconsequent in her (and perhaps our) mad pursuit of this widely touted but elusive elixir. The meanings of words and actions dissolve in the turmoil. We are not ruthless, we are not even responsible for much; we are simply a country/world/universe, Lady Gaga postulates, of weird, bullied people hoping to find a path through the chaos and a way to feel good about ourselves.

WHY DWELL ON Riefenstahl and Lady Gaga? Riefenstahl provides a high-water mark of ruthless ambition in a self-proclaimed artist; Lady Gaga shows us a partial, updated version of a similar urgency for fame, accompanied by a strong wish to be, or be seen as, both wildly out there and yet kind and caring. (No biographies yet exist that might offer a fuller backstory of her rise.) Together Riefenstahl and Lady Gaga offer us a thought lesson, a way to ponder how much drive, not to mention how strong a stomach, is required to pursue huge success.

But the other, less predictable reason to look at these two lives is that they help us picture the distance—the orders of magnitude—between the profoundly ambitious and the typically more modest artist or craftsperson. The majority of very talented, serious, very successful artists live a less destructive trajectory than Riefenstahl's and a less insane one than Germanotto's. What ruthlessness they possess is better defined as the strenuous work they do to keep their focus and to eschew many normal distractions—including certain kinds of diffuse interests, wool gathering, or generosity with time—that divert the rest of us. While each person is different, I imagine that many are inclined to be thoughtful about the trades they make and to acknowledge sacrifice and consequence.

I remember my colleague Leston Havens lecturing graduate students and young doctors in our hospital, pointing out to them how decent, self-aware people tend to be tied in knots by their small character failings, while their less self-aware counterparts barely notice their own, much more egregious lapses. And my guess is that many readers of this chapter, rather than too unconcerned, will be too apprehensive about small bits of risk or self-assertion or of taking some parenting or family time for their own work, that they will too quickly worry they are being ruthless when they are not.

The great reason for exploring the extremes is so that we can think about where we want to position ourselves and why. But lest we get carried away with the virtues of such hypothetical moderation, there's a wonderful reminder for us in a line in Robert Penn Warren's novel *All the King's Men*, where the narrator posits that a man's virtue may be "but a defect in his desire."

IV

WHILE RIEFENSTAHL WAS weaving her thread upon Hitler's loom, Thomas Mann (1875–1955), the German novelist who in 1929 won the Nobel prize, was busy fleeing Nazism, first to Switzerland in 1933, then on to the United States in 1939.

Mann, too, weighed in on ruthlessness, and his observations lead us close to the heart of the matter where art-making itself is concerned. I earlier asked why ruthlessness is a question for all artists and craftspeople, not simply the most ambitious. The significant answer concerns the way an artist must "look" at the world and at his or her own work. Much of art is about translating close observation. The horses in the field become the horses on the cave wall. And so the capacity to observe frankly, sometimes ruthlessly, becomes a deeply important component of artistry.

Mann states it well when he writes:

The look that one directs at things, both outward and inward, as an artist is not the same as that with which one would regard the same as a man, but at once colder and more passionate. As a man, you might be well-disposed, patient, loving, positive, and have a wholly uncritical inclination to look upon everything as all right, but as artist your daemon constrains you to "observe," to take note, lightning fast and with hurtful malice, of every detail that in the literary sense would be characteristic, distinctive, significant, opening insights, typifying the race, the social or the psychological mode, recording all as mercilessly as though you had no human relationship to the observed object whatever.[19]

MANN GRANTS RUTHLESSNESS direct relationship to creating excellent work. Though perhaps too severe in his manner, he tells us something true. Isn't "recording all as mercilessly as though you had no human relationship to the observed object whatever" a restatement of Arabella's admonition to Jude, and of ruthlessness? The artist's eye must resist any invitation to look away, must resist the unconsidered reflex of ruth. The claim "at once colder and more passionate" deftly holds two necessary opposites. Your job as an artist is neither to spare the pig nor, Riefenstahl style, to smear lipstick on it and call it by some other name, but to look, act, feel, and transform all that is bearable and unbearable into your work. In this sense, Jude's failure is not simply that he cannot stand to make the animal suffer, but that he cannot bear to suffer the feelings that harming the animal will awaken in him.

In May of 1962, the Guggenheim Museum held a retrospective of Philip Guston's paintings. Mayer describes how Guston almost cancelled it because he was terrified of seeing his work en masse, of feeling so exposed, judged, and found wanting that it would kill off his hope for himself as a painter. But he changed his mind. And while the event was extremely difficult for him, and shocking, he "recovered" gradually. "It took me about a year to get started painting again," he said, "and stop brooding about the work. But it was of great value to me. I think I became more ruthless with myself in the work following."[20]

It's frustrating not to know exactly what he means here, what he could tell us about the shift of becoming more ruthless with himself. But certainly he alludes to how difficult it can be to be as bold, self-demanding, and detached as originality requires—to renounce your easy satisfaction in your hard-won productions, overcome intense attachment, and put quality ahead of fondness. I remember once seeing the stack of forty or fifty contact prints, each containing thirty-six photos in miniature (an entire roll of film in the predigital era), that a *National Geographic* photographer had shot in order to get a single image that satisfied him. The pile of pictures bore witness to how hard he had been willing to work to translate his visual observation into something that held up as a photograph. I similarly learned from my father how relentlessly a writer must cross out words, toss pages, and tear up drafts in order to create one fine short story. (Though his daily laboring was ruthless enough, he once burned the single manuscript of a novel that displeased him.)

Some people give up on mastery because they don't grasp how rigorous the observing process actually is, how demanding of multiple tries and courage, so they fault themselves for not achieving more sooner or working more rapidly.

V

LILLIAN HELLMAN'S MEMOIR, *Pentimento*, long ago fell from grace after many, most famously the novelist and critic Mary McCarthy, challenged its veracity and called Hellman "a dishonest writer." (McCarthy's unforgettable line, now a cultural trope: "every word she writes is a lie including 'and' and 'the.'") Still, I remember as a young woman loving a story in it called "Turtle," which ponders the ruth/ruthless question and the whole larger artist's dilemma of attachment and detachment, and I recently reread it. Whether or not it hews close to any facts, the story offers strong psychological commentary on the failure of ruthlessness in art-making.

Killing one's own meat is something Hellman favors but unexpectedly finds unbearable when confronted on her farm one day with a snapping turtle that won't die. She tells her lover, Dashiell Hammett ("Dash"), who has trapped and attempted to slaughter the reptile after it lamed one of their dogs, "You know very well that I help with the butchering of the animals here and don't like talk about how distasteful killing is by people who are willing to eat what is killed for them."[21] But after witnessing the effort the decapitated reptile (head dangling from neck by a thread) makes to escape from their kitchen, to drag its bloody, dead self down the steps and back toward their pond, she is overcome. Feeling that its primeval tenacity has earned it the right to be buried rather than eaten, she tells Dash that she doesn't want its flesh for soup. Hammett dismisses her scruples and refuses to assist with grave-digging, so, in the middle of the night, a whisky-emboldened Hellman stumbles forth with her shovel and buries the carcass—too shallowly, it turns out, for within days animals dig it up and eat it. Or so the story goes.

Veracious or not, *Pentimento* became a best seller. The book's success was no accident, since feminism was gathering steam, and Hellman offered one of the few glimpses yet available in that now-almost-inconceivably-sexist American world of the early 1970s, of a way for a woman to live that seemingly wasn't subservient and submissive. While we know in retrospect that Hellman's portrait of her own boldness is often more wish than fact, in the historical moment her fudged self-portrayal held great appeal. She put herself before her readers as an aging woman who had lived hard—artistically, sexually, sensually, independently, courageously—achieving great success with plays like *The Little Foxes* and *The Children's Hour* and yet not compromising her integrity in the process. And, in the United States in 1973, such a public image of female was anomalous.

The "who kills the meat" dilemma in "Turtle" figures into *our* discussion because it sheds further light on ruthlessness by noting that it has long been superficially gendered. Outside of that pariah, the abandoning mother, and the occasional portrayal of the political female—Cleopatra, Lady Macbeth, and the two Lear daughters come quickly to mind, as do fairy tales of diverse witches and stepmothers—the lion's share of ruthlessness has traditionally been assigned to men, a split that has historically held true as well where art-making is involved. One hasn't traditionally associated ruthlessness and the female artist, however incorrect the lapse. But then, until a slow, oft-interrupted turnaround began sometime in the 19th century, female artists in the United States (outside of those pursuing the "domestic" arts) have been relatively few and far between and largely scorned if they tried to cross into a center stage of the public world.

Whether one reads her lines or between them, Hellman's presentation of herself as a bold, tough, successful woman playwright (and perhaps, not coincidentally, an unmarried woman without children) seems inseparable from her meat-killing injunction. While she never directly speaks it, her self-portrayal is a testimony to her assumption that the two are necessarily linked. And, as Hardy points out with Jude, and Hellman enacts with her quandary of the turtle, killing one's meat correctly, and in Hellman's case eating it with appropriate gusto, demands a certain ruthlessness. One must not allow one's empathy for the creature to interfere with the task at hand.

Yet in "Turtle" Hellman endears herself to her readers by both knowing the rule and finding herself unexpectedly swayed from her fidelity to it. When one recalls her historic moment and the staggering difficulty for a female playwright in the 1930s, '40s, and '50s to elbow her way to the top of the theater world's male-dominated heap, one can only assume that at times she identified more than she could say with the battle-weary reptile who, though bested, crawled forth, head dangling by a thread.

And perhaps she also felt remorse for the fellow creatures she'd snapped at and lamed as she blundered along. Most of all, she intuited that to write successful memoirs (*Pentimento* was one of several she authored) for the rising generation of women, she would have to present herself as having somehow worked out the ruth/ruthlessness quandary enough to succeed in the then male public world.

But what if we read her story momentarily as a fable about her own effort to write a memoir, and about whether or not to hew ruthlessly to the more literal or more complex truth? Then her predicament becomes a psychological one about art-making instead of soup-making. In this reading, her compassion for the turtle would be for herself as fictionalizer, the writer self who wants to let that maimed creature—the ugly, imperfect, ambiguous truth—escape out the back door and earn a quiet burial. (And yet, as Freud observed about unconscious conflict, it inhabits a shallow grave and won't stay buried.) By this interpretation, one can read her struggle as a battle between the part of her that would rigorously write a memoir of facts versus the part of her that finds truths about her life discordant with her purpose, or finds her lived past unbearable, and the process of retrieving and writing about it overwhelmingly painful—perhaps shameful or politically incorrect, perhaps sad, perhaps brimming with regret, perhaps simply inconvenient. The writer spares the "turtle" self the final indignity by creating a better, braver, and more memorable Hellman than the real one who lived the actual life. In this sense, Hellman's failure to accurately recount her history is a failure of adequate artistic ruthlessness.

Still and all, Hellman enjoyed her fame. And maybe she fictionalized to increase her odds of having the memoir make her more famous—which it did. (So famous that in 1976, over seventy, she posed in a widely published Blackglama fur advertisement, wearing nothing but the coat.) Maybe her particular ruthlessness was not in the service of her art qua art, but for the sake of a captivating last act. Maybe she lulled herself into believing the fiction was the truth and wrote the words she sensed would bring her most acclaim. Another famous story in the collection, "Julia," about Hellman's claim to have risked her life as a courier for money to help a woman named Julia save lives from the Nazis, was long ago unmasked as a tale Hellman plagiarized and never lived.

By the time Hellman came to writing memoirs, she had lost whatever stomach she may earlier have possessed to separate the self-protecting woman from the artist, to look upon herself coldly, at least with pen in hand. Obviously, memoir offers more of a predicament than fiction in this regard, because the object of the gaze is the self, and there is nowhere to hide. The fiction writer's screen is exactly what the memoirist claims to forsake. And perhaps what ultimately is moving in "Turtle" is some resonance of the author's invisible yet present struggle with this failure of writerly courage. Someone declared at Hellman's own graveside, "She was awful but she was worth it." And I suspect the quip's truth was in the mourner's grasp of the artist's wish to have been other than how she was, and of the way that wish created a lovable dimension in a very difficult woman—a view separate from the more glamorous one Hellman sought to project as herself.

But, if any of these conjectures about Hellman's narrative of the turtle is on the mark, it underscores again how ruthlessness serves different masters. The compelling requirement, which a jury of her peers suggests Hellman failed, is for ruthlessness— here meaning some combination of honesty and rigor—to labor in the service of the art-making itself. In retrospect, I think this message is the one my father wanted to convey when he dug out his copy of Thomas Hardy, and the one I pass along here.

Finally, now, when I reflect back yet again on our conversation, on my father's life, and his insistence on holding on to Jude's perspective and on to Arabella's, I realize he offered a second lesson perhaps more subtle, but equally important: Being able to kill the pig, yet also experiencing your remorse, holding on to both sides of the "ruth" dilemma, living its complexity—as he did in his stories, and in his life—is a strenuous yet worthwhile undertaking.

CHAPTER 8

going public

I

TO UNDERSTAND THE psychological quandaries of going public, I want to begin by returning briefly, once again, to the matter of privacy. Artists generally need privacy in order to create, and as I've noted, what constitutes adequate privacy varies by person and time. Solitude quickly becomes isolation when it oversteps one's desires. But most artists need to feel that they and their work won't be examined prematurely and, certainly, won't be ambushed unfinished by ridiculing eyes. You might go out and invite various people to critique a piece in progress, even knowing they're unlikely to view it with sympathy, exactly because you feel there's necessary information in their opinion. But, if you've invited them, however unpleasant the response, your experience is likely preferable to what you would feel if they impulsively offered up the same critiques unsolicited.

Someone making art needs privacy in part because the process of creation makes many people feel vulnerable, sometimes exquisitely so, particularly since the work frequently emerges in a jumble of mixed-up small parts that you can only assemble gradually, or in a wet lumpy mound that requires patient sculpting. When people feel prematurely revealed or exposed, they often experience great discomfort and find themselves babbling apologetically, seeking to reassure by laying out the distance they have yet to travel. It is in part this babble-as-smoke-screen to cover exposure and the resulting, distracting, unhappy self-consciousness that privacy seeks to shelter.

But even more significantly, privacy grants us permission to turn our attention inward without interruption. As I described earlier, in order to concentrate, think, and fantasize, we need to feel we're in a safe enough space that we can lower our vigilance, stop monitoring our environment, and allow ourselves to refocus on the happenings within our own minds. There are times interruptions feel merciful, but many more when they disrupt our effort to flesh out an inchoate notion.

If the process of creation is the foal, than privacy is the mare edging around to place herself between the newborn creature and the wind. For some, adequate privacy might be a door that can be shut or a pair of earplugs or earphones; for others, a quiet library carrel or a table in a café where you are surrounded by the talk of strangers. But the physical specs entwine with psychological need. Many people working on a piece need to curtain themselves from a sometimes overwhelming feeling of scrutiny they carry in their own minds.

Elizabeth Bishop found the privacy she needed for a while by "ex-patting" herself to Brazil. She made a new life for herself far from America and far from everything familiar in her old one. Her lover built her a studio that stood apart from the bustling main house, itself up in the hills of rural Brazil. On the wall of her workroom, Bishop tacked up photographs of Charles Baudelaire and of her close poet friends Marianne Moore and Robert Lowell. She removed herself from public view and then carefully chose the eyes that could see her as she worked—and as she lived. In part, Bishop traveled to Brazil to pursue a romance with Lota de Macedo Soares, the woman whose home provided her one of the few real havens she found during her orphaned, peripatetic life. It seems she needed the privacy of exile in order to grant herself sustained intimacy. And the relationship, at least in its early years, helped her become a more grounded person and poet. It didn't hurt that in the beginning Lota had adequate wealth to relieve Bishop from her habitual dread of not being able to support herself. Bishop, so emotionally deprived as a girl, craved care, and for a while Lota provided that as well. She nursed her, doling out tranquilizers and Antabuse, and helped her struggle with her often debilitating drinking. What's more, she offered Bishop a vibrant domestic life loud with the chattering of cooks and gardeners, the cries of babies, parrots, and cats, the rush of hard rain on tropical foliage, visits from neighbors, overnight guests from everywhere, and endless daytrips and exotic vistas.

Brazil enabled other important privacies that helped Bishop thrive. Her biographer Brett Millier notes that the distance itself helped her get free of the pressures of "poetic ambition" that had contributed to her misery in her native land. She felt inadequate and compared herself unfavorably to all the poets she met. In her own eyes she continually fell short, even after considerable success. She couldn't stop chastising herself for how she spent her time, how slowly she worked, how ill-suited she felt for the template "poet's life" of public readings and teaching. She believed that for her to be a "real" poet, her technique and subject matter would have to be different from what they were. Her style was carefully formed, straightforward, and accessible. She liked writing about places and things and about what she observed around her. But that wasn't good enough, or so she feared. Her aesthetic preferences, strongly felt, troubled her and at times drew criticism from contemporaries who believed poetry should deal either with intimate confession, or with more abstract symbols, or with the big social and political issues of the day.[1]

In Brazil, Bishop could separate herself from the jangle and static caused by this constant worry of what others were thinking or doing, and from her fantasies of how they were outstripping her. Once she turned down the volume, she not only breathed more freely, but also seemed to become more centered and at ease—at least for a while. The actual distance between Brazil and New England aided her. The studio helped. But such concrete aids were not the only ones needed by her, or by many people, since much of one's sense of privacy is psychological. Our own minds are our first public, and they can be as harsh an audience as we encounter. One antidote is intimacies like Bishop's with Lota, or between the Wordsworths, and between Bishop and Lowell. The support, praise, and encouragement of some close relationships can create a baffle that tempers the harsher sounds.

Psychotherapy serves a similar function for some by offering support as well as perspective on feelings of shame, disappointment, and doubt and by defanging the more vicious and intimidating among the internal critics. Ideally, you want to understand their concerns yet quiet them, soothe their worries, and invite them to take a long nap by the fire while you draft. Internal criticism, when not over-the-top or too strident, is useful to art-making. The kvetching chorus labors to safeguard your wish to do good work; it helps to keep you at the ornery task, to push your brain into finding a surer melody or better rhymes. Sometimes, we will work just as hard polishing a piece without self-criticism or fear to prod us, but often, as Samuel Johnson suggested, "the sight of the gallows clears the mind." Our brains use the internal criticisms to find the flaws before they get found by others, to inspect the product several times over. One goes public first in one's mind as a way of preparing, as best one can, for the loss of control in the real event.

Still, it's a matter of balance. The positive function of internal critics fails when the nattering becomes too loud, unnuanced, or intimidating to let the work go forward, or when it negates the value of what we've done. Particular criticisms can be useful, while overarching condemnations are noxious. And, self-knowledge is essential to help you sort when you're in useful territory, when not. Obviously, no self-criticism is useful unless you counterbalance it well with positive notices when you've created something that pleases and excites you. (You also need privacy to enjoy your pleasure in your work without having the good feeling prematurely undone by your own critics or someone else's.)

Because so much of the creative process is outside of immediate conscious control, a writer aims in a direction—in pursuit of a thought, an image, or a sound—and then both actively thinks and passively awaits the words, scribbles them down, assesses them, edits them, alters them, eliminates some or all, and begins again. (Jennifer Egan, the Pulitzer Prize–winning author of *A Visit from the Goon Squad*, among other works, has said that her novels may go through fifty or sixty drafts.)[2] The larger piece builds in this uneven fashion because it emerges from different levels of thought and feeling. The unconscious parts of the mind, like rivers, seek their own paths, and the more conscious thoughts attempt to engineer dikes and levees to guide them. Settling into a regular process of working can help gradually to regulate your responses to yourself. Ideally, you want to go completely into the work, and then stand back, so you move among creator, critic, and editor in a rhythm that facilitates rather than paralyzes you.

Indeed, one way you can recognize when it is time to show your work in progress to another person is when you lose that self-observing rhythm and come to a standstill in your own effort—when you cannot move forward, you have lost your pleasure, and you are weary. Such feelings often signal that you've spent too much time alone with the process or the piece, and you need someone else's appraisal, applause, or suggestion for revisions.

II

WHATEVER ACCOMMODATION YOU manage, one day the more solitary phase ends. You finish the book or poem or painting or musical composition. And however you have carefully arranged geography, furniture, and psyche to create a sheltering space, the internal sojourn is now over. It is time to reenter the world. The leap may sound straightforward, but if you've been lingering deep inside yourself, the attendant feelings of that reentry tend to be more challenging than any simple narrative implies. Part of you feels exhilarated to have finished your piece; part of you feels frightened or even more vulnerable than while you were working. You may also feel exhausted. Or like some half-blinded creature lumbering unhappily from its dark cave into midday sun. The glare disorients you; you blink a lot. It is tempting to turn around.

Going public with your art is adulthood writ large: There is excitement, satisfaction, praise; there is also criticism, disappointment, and embarrassment. And while it may not be literally true, the feelings seem ratcheted up a notch or two when they involve bringing creative efforts to an audience. Whatever happens, the external response is largely beyond your control.

AMONG THE PERILS along our pilgrim's route, the towering, unstable boulder that blocks the turnoff onto the final miles is this matter of going public. Of course, not for everyone, yet plenty of people get this far in the path and no farther. And while we would be comforted to imagine a gate at the end of the trek that opens and shuts impartially according to the quality of our product, or, even more wishfully, the sincerity of our effort, no such luck. The tired pilgrim, worn out but perhaps heartened, even energized, by news of an end to the journey, pulls himself or herself over a large rise only to learn that there is no gate. Instead, as in some cosmic video game, a massive boulder careens about—opening the way, blocking the way—almost more whimsically than can be borne. And those attempting to traverse the crushing passage must develop strategies and quick steps to gain what control they can.

The metaphorical boulder represents many things. It is the actual obstacles: the difficulties linking work to market or venue, attracting positive attention, pursuing sales. It is also the sun overriding the lamplight: the moment when the dreams have to bang into the glare of real. To keep working, the mind must, at least at moments, create a glimmer of a receptive audience, so it fantasizes about understanding, approval, or success. These hopeful fantasies work like some mix of stimulants and opiates; they summon Xanadu and dull the pain; at the same time, they help keep the artist printing and reprinting the image through the onerous stretches until it looks right. They don't substitute for our desire to create the work for its own sake, but they brace that wish and help sustain it.

Coaches similarly attempt to cultivate "visualizations" to spur athletes. *Visualize yourself succeeding at the triple lutz. Visualize yourself having the Olympic gold medal placed around your neck.* This useful concretization of hope is as old as the human mind. Some have claimed that the cave paintings, to return to a favorite motif, represented the hunter's effort to visualize his much-needed prey as abundant and at hand, perhaps even magically lured closer by the painted image itself.

Sometimes the art-maker's daydreams are as blatant as the teenage guitarist's seeing himself on stage in place of his idol, pounding chords as his audience swoons. Other times, they are the more low-key imagining of a mentor examining your well-made bowl and offering a compliment.

Psychologically, for many artists, attempting to go public is the great test, the stuff of night sweats and elation. But going public is also often quiet, undramatic, sometimes even utterly mundane; certainly for most of us it begins that way. You hand a watercolor you've painted to a friend and she hangs it in her hall-way. An audience can be and often is, early on, one person—as when I show some pages of an early draft of an essay to my husband, or when a sculptor friend invites me in to look at a piece in progress. Once again, a sympathetic friend or mentor is a good beginning, someone you respect who will appreciate your work, perhaps nudge it a little, but without too much quibble.

The first professional audience for a writer (beyond graduate school for those who attend it) is likely to be an agent or an editor. But, as Jonathan Galassi, the publisher at Farrar, Straus and Giroux, observed about editors, their function is often like that of a friend who offers more powerful encouragement thanks to the authority of title:

> *I think the real thing an editor does for a writer is to look him in the eye and affirm that he exists, that his work is genuine, acceptable, true to himself . . . As I've gone along in my trade, I've come to feel that authors need less line-editing and more hand-holding, more empathy and authentically affectionate response. The editor's essential job is to give the writer permission to be her essential self.*[3]

I REMEMBER YEARS ago the psychologist and biographer Margaret Brenman-Gibson telling me of how she got stymied and blocked trying to write a biography of the playwright Clifford Odets. She'd done her research, but she could not write, and as she became more discouraged, she couldn't even stay in her chair long enough to try. Finally, her friend and colleague Erik Erikson told her that he would spend one afternoon a week sitting with her in a room in Austen Riggs, the hospital where they both worked, so she could write. And so they did, and in 1981, more than a decade and a half from the time she started her research, she published her book, which was very well received. Erikson offered her a generous dose of the empathy and hand-holding Galassi describes, and my guess is that by doing so he also inserted himself into her mind as her first audience. He both got her to commit to a structure and freed her to work.

Sometimes, however carefully you pick, your first audience might be the wrong one. Around 1994, after months of struggle and feeling completely raw and uncertain, I showed the first four chapters of my first book to a ferocious mentor, who read them and pronounced—bitterly, angrily—in her thick eastern European accent, "Tear them up and start again." On some level, she may have been correct. She was a multi-degreed scholar who lived for ideas and literature and had fierce standards. I was writing nonfiction outside the academy, thus not in a league she favored. Still, I held her in high esteem, and she had across some years genuinely aided me in my efforts to learn to write, so her words initially ripped out my liver. It was hard not to do her bidding, even as I recognized her manner as outrageous. When I found a little distance and stitched myself up, I realized that I'd struggled way too much to toss the pages in the fireplace, or to light the match. Instead, I asked another writer to read them who—lucky for me—offered strong encouragement. And perhaps learning to ignore someone whose opinion carried high value during a long apprenticeship is, in its way, also a part of going public. Her response taught me nothing useful about the chapters, but it did teach me to seek more than one reader before reaching any conclusions about what I might not be seeing.

Our exchange highlights how the act of going public is also challenging because it sometimes requires you to defend yourself. Just as you need to open yourself to thoughtful criticism, you also have to be ready to fight to protect what you believe is right in your work, and to make your way through the rebuffs and rejections. Not only do you have to take your own side, you also have to say what you mean. And consequently, you will be seen both trying and failing, holding your ground and sometimes being dead wrong. Such exposure is not often pleasant, but it is a definite part of going public. And, once again, it contradicts the simple wished-for narrative, the middle school tale of merit recognized. You write the paragraph, the great teacher in the sky hands out the "A." Going public, you write the paragraph, and the teacher is AWOL. In his place are an ever-evolving cast of characters—some beneficent, even too generous, others malicious, or inebriated, still others ill. Like figures in Bunyan, or perhaps in a sixteenth-century Flemish crucifixion crowd, they may assist you, or they may just guffaw and throw stuff. You want to make your way? It's up to you to amuse and distract the whole mob, to do whatever it takes to keep them from making you flee.

As well as picking the wrong person, it is easy to pick the wrong venue when you take your piece out into the world. And herein is an oft-repeated but still important kernel: You are most likely to have a reasonable experience going public if you pick an outlet appropriate to your work. If you rent Carnegie Hall for an evening, and hire and rehearse a trio to perform your latest composition, not only do you need to invite—way ahead and very nicely—the press and anyone significant in the music world who might even remotely come, but you also need to have roped in enough friends to fill the empty seats. Otherwise, it's better to go for a more modest space. It's not that overreaching is bad, it's just something to be done handily, because it can feel really unpleasant when it backfires. It's great to have a grand hall in your sights. But if you want to get there, you do best if you pitch yourself at a plausible level, and do your ground work. You will feel better, and you will be more likely to find a receptive audience. If you please that audience, you are on your way to the next, more challenging place.

The venue rules today are complicated and changing constantly. I recently spoke with a young writer who talked about the enormous pressure on her, as a young artist, to create a blog with a substantial following before a conventional publisher would buy her work. This is no mean feat, since the Internet, while a huge force, is an erratic one. You can make the video that wins the YouTube-hits lottery and go from unknown to too known in a day. Or, more often, you may create a website but feel unsure how to invite traffic. You can send news of your latest gallery show to 1,000 friends on Facebook, only to remember that 90 percent of them live in other states or other countries.

You might say that the Internet functions like a scratch ticket that sometimes perplexes or defeats and every so often yields up unexpected prizes. When our younger son produced, in Massachusetts, a vinyl recording for his locally known punk band, three separate stores in Japan ordered copies—because they'd found and listened to the songs on MySpace. I would never have been able to guess that stores on the other side of the world would lead the pack buying his music. At the same time, many art-makers are baffled by the Internet, and even famous artists find that its easy piracy irks them more than it assists them. I suspect in ten or twenty years everyone will understand better how to use it, but now many of us, older neophytes especially, feel as if we've been blindfolded and spun about.

One thought would be to dabble in the types of social media that you find most *sympathique*, and to eschew those that make you miserable. *The New York Times Book Review* ran an essay by Anne Trubek exploring various contemporary writers' feelings about Twittering their fans.[4] Some enjoyed it; some didn't. Some found it increased their connection to their readers in a positive way; others felt that it diminished their readers' pleasure in their work by confusing the story and the storyteller. Make your own experiments. See what you think.

The Internet and social media notwithstanding, much art remains local, something I think we tend to forget. We are encouraged to, and most of us do, focus disproportionately on the small number of works that break through and become broadly acclaimed. But the group of players in that megastar world is small, and the rest of us gain much more satisfaction seeking our publics more pragmatically.

I recall one summer night on the island in Maine we visit each summer, watching a play called *The Little Locksmith* that an island director, John Wulp, and a novelist from the next island, Susan Minot, had adapted from a memoir by Katharine Butler Hathaway. Hathaway was a child with a crooked back, who, on the basis of a doctor's less-than-sound medical wisdom, had spent five years of her early twentieth-century childhood strapped to a board, unable to move, with the aim that her back could be deterred from its warping inclination, and she would be spared life as "a hunchback." It didn't work. Wulp, Minot, and Linda Hunt, the actress who visited to play the part, all have international reputations, so in that sense the play was not local. But the story is unlikely to find, was not meant for, a global audience; it needed Maine.

The production worked brilliantly as a night of theater for those of us in attendance on the island because we could feel it down to our toes; because it was ours. It was as if in some uncanny way, though the details were fresh and surprising, we already knew much about the story. The drama was set in Hathaway's childhood summer house in Castine, a nearby town on the Maine coast, and as audience we could more or less look from the theater seats out onto the same ocean, trees, rocks, fish houses, and fog as the author describes. We sat rapt in the tiny community room, with its folding metal chairs in rows, and with the single spotlight, and a lone woman seated on a stool narrating her lost childhood and her Maine coast life. It isn't that I—or likely anyone present—would claim to have lived in the world she described. But simply through our intimacy with our own locale, we grasped the tale's veracity: the way its material and emotional vestiges lingered into the audience's shared present. We felt we could confirm its truth from the physical bits of it we could touch around us so many years later. The woman speaking seemed at once here, and yet a ghost of there, and this doubleness made for moments of full goose flesh.

III

As I MENTIONED, the first psychological task in going public is to shift emotional gears and move from a place of solitude and inner-directed thought to one where you agree to have the work seen, and thus, in fantasy if not reality, to be seen yourself. Lucky are those who possess thick shin guards and the ability to tune out the inclemencies of others. I suspect such insulation is not often granted in quantity to art-makers whose permeable membranes feed their creativity but leave them, well, permeable. Certainly, there are some who come complete with Gore-Tex, and many others who compensate with bluster and bravado, and maybe marijuana. But for the rest of us, simply finding ways to endure the hail of our own angst, together with the real critiques and rebuffs, requires as much psychological effort as we can muster. (Ironically, there are also people who feel considerable psychic upset when their work meets with success or positive reception, and more than a few people have a touch of that experience. Very bad and very good news, however opposite, tends to rock us, and sometimes to challenge our basic sense of ourselves. But given a choice . . .)

One aspect of this private-public transition is the shift of expressive focus. Often, you need to learn how to talk about what you've done. (Tom Waits equates the work of talking publically about a new album to "doing the dishes." You've enjoyed the meal—of creating and producing—and now you've got to scrape plates and clean up.)[5] The particular task for the art-maker or craftsperson is that the part of the brain that creates and the part that can describe are often poorly linked. Not for everyone; I know a very successful nonfiction writer who can regale all comers with tales about her topic long before she's worked out its path. She is an extroverted and gifted narrator. And thinking aloud helps her find her own direction more clearly. But many other people find that language transition more difficult. Like trying to describe New York City in a single sentence, you stutter, "Big . . . lots of people . . . tall buildings." And your interlocutor wonders what loser he's encountered, and looks longingly toward the wine bar. Sometimes for me it feels as if particular thoughts are in a vault, where only the writer, not the speaker, enters. I've now made enough pitches to publishers, and given enough talks about my books, to know that I can do good patter once I've made a transition, but there's an initial disconnect between the woman who speaks on the radio or in a lecture hall and the one who thinks and writes. The writer is more hesitant, a little lost in thought, more constantly reconsidering. The public speaker is more definite, more focused on being succinct, and on interacting with others.

The wish that opposes the wish for privacy is the need *not* to be alone and unseen. You go public because you want to be recognized as someone with something to offer. You want to be told your contribution is valued. It's a completely normal communal desire. Self-respect and self-esteem do not often fare well in isolation. They are earned through the sum of our actions and activities with other people. For art-makers, that means having your work seen and evaluated, and maybe even having it sell. However unlikely grand success with bundles of money, you can know real satisfaction in going public, often in the form of homeopathic thimblefuls of the above. There is also the satisfaction of making an effort; the vitality of taking part in the market; the pleasure of hope and good responses, which for writers include the occasional favorable review, a lively conversation with a radio host who genuinely wants to converse, or an enthusiastic letter or email from a stranger. Furthermore, gaining an audience, feeling valued, recursively strengthens your own belief in your work, and sometimes also its quality.

Then, too, there is the wish to have something to sell. Years ago, one cold, rainy March day while my husband, sons, and I were standing in a market in Crete, a friend expanded his arms toward all the impoverished farmers who filled the place, each one having arrived with a small armload of thin asparagus, wild mustard greens, or early onions. It was off-season for tourists; meanwhile, the winter had emptied people's cupboards and small savings. Vendors seemed subdued. "The truth is," our friend announced dramatically, slightly imploringly in his Greek-accented English, "everyone just wants to have something to sell." The remark seemed so right, at once particular and cosmic, that it has lingered with me. And, on some simple, straightforward level, apart from all the other various fantasies they might possess, artists who go public are often people who want to have something to sell, and who hope their art can make up some portion of their wares. (Sometimes, as until recently with Burning Man, or in some parts of the punk music world, or with graffiti art, art-makers protest the commoditization of art by offering their work for free or as something to be seen or heard but not possessed.) Yet for many of us, hawking the products of one's own thought and imagination has a delicious organic quality to it. As with the clipped bounty of a sheep's wool, or the cucumber picked from its vine, something has seemingly grown from nothing, has been spun from the mind or from raw elements, and now takes a material form, and can be sold. This alchemic satisfaction is by no means the whole story, but it's not insignificant.

I remember reading John Updike's description of the delight it gave him to hold the first copy he received of a new book, and to place it on his shelf. And certainly there's something about the heft of the pages that is gratifying, that suggests that your great expense of time has not simply drifted into the general fog. When you turn away and return, the volume is still there. The mind's processes are ephemeral. Images, thoughts, feelings race about, responding to the sensation of the moment, appearing and disappearing, often leaving no trace—rather the way dreams dissipate so quickly on awakening. The objects of art are the mind's brief moments captured and bronzed, allowed to linger past their time.

But my memory of the armloads of greens also brings us back to the need sometimes to use your elbows so you can resist the crush of the crowd. If you want to get your work out of your drawer, you have to enter the marketplace, and when you do, you need to be prepared for its brisk, pushy approach. So you want to publish? Or get a gallery? Or perform? Make your case. Justify yourself. Why should we host your performance, sell your painting, publish your book? The piece itself may be compelling, but a lot of stuff is compelling. What kind of audience can you deliver? What makes yours worth my dollar? The marketplace simply asks the questions that are within its domain. They are not personal, or intended to send you scurrying even when they do. They are the buzz, slap, and ruckus created by people trying to survive by selling. You need to find your way with them. It's just made harder because often the skills you need in the market are quite different from the ones you use while you work. You strip off your own defenses to create, and then must reassume them to enter the world. And many people find that dual effort challenging, not to mention unpleasant, difficult, or simply undo-able. Others take to it like Brer Rabbit to the briar patch.

As I've noted, some terrible artists are terrific self-promoters. And vice versa. Occasionally, a single person possesses both qualities. Walt Whitman was not just an extraordinary poet but also his own best tout. When Whitman first printed up *Leaves of Grass*, he sent a copy to Ralph Waldo Emerson—who loved it and recognized his talent. Emerson wrote Whitman back a letter that included the line "I greet you at the beginning of a great career." Whitman then embossed Emerson's plaudit onto the spine of each copy of the collection—without asking Emerson. The elder man was vexed, but the deed was done.[6] And while Whitman more than deserved the praise, no cultural observer would claim predictable correlation between the ability to gather blurbs or media face time and the quality of the work.

Many artists who might possess the skills still feel that there's something icky about promoting their work. Partly it's embarrassment (*How can I say this is worth buying?*); partly a kind of entitlement (*Why should I, the artist, have to?*); partly a time concern (*On top of my day job, this too?*); partly an anxiety from not knowing how or what to do (*I only have three friends on Facebook, and they are real friends and I've already given them free tickets to my concert*). God invented publicists to help artists with cash in hand get around the dilemma by parceling out some of the work. Otherwise, for better or worse, it's ever more in our own hands.

Occasionally, a person gets lucky in her friends or kin. Or her promise attracts well-placed mentors. The more you read of Elizabeth Bishop's letters and her life, the clearer it becomes that her career was greatly aided, her public access facilitated, by both Margaret Moore and Robert Lowell. Lowell, well connected in the literary world, made Bishop his mission. He turned his considerable charm, energy, and status in their shared world to finding her grants, fellowships, residencies, teaching positions, calling critical attention to her work, and suggesting to literary editors that they publish her.

But such large assists are rare, and even the best help only goes so far. Unless you want to keep all you produce only for your own eyes, you have to cultivate the salesperson in you as well as the art-maker. At the least, you have to recognize that you need both selves. The job of the salesperson is to summon enough bravado to bear the market in its own terms, to understand that the noise is impersonal, the abrasions are circumstantial. There's

a lot of jostling and even the occasional fight, but whether ex-
hilarating or terrible, they are not about you, or not fully, a
truth almost impossible to remember when it's your flesh that's
scratched. They are more about survival and profit, and in a
broader sense about public power, opinion, taste, and style. They
often concern cultural fantasies that have agendas of their own,
and that are larger than any one of our small lives.

IV

EXPERIENCES, LIKE TEMPERAMENTS, are very varied, and sometimes art-makers have less ambivalent—even pure good—times
when they dive into the fray. I crossed paths with a lay scholar
who had worked on a nonfiction book for two decades, which,
when she published it, met with great success. The book sold well
and won awards. She garnered offers from all quarters, and she
burst from obscurity to prominence with the ease of someone
sticking a hand through a paper screen. When I asked her how
going public had been for her, she answered sincerely that it had
been all good. She had felt able to relish the attention, the reviews,
the high sales, the success, and the opportunities. You might say
she'd known (and earned) the pleasure of delivering to the market
something well grown, fully ripened and unblemished, at exactly
the moment the market wanted what she was selling.

Yet her tale is atypical. Most people, even when they meet
some success, encounter many disappointments. And the fact that

they come with the territory doesn't soften their edges. Unless you are extraordinarily realistic and rational, or have set your sites with great accuracy, or have produced something unusually fine, or possess the very hottest item sought, you may be in for a reception that does not match your hopes. Disappointment is common in artists' experience of going public, and it feels like the proverbial grandmother with the single eye in the middle of her forehead whom, Lyndon Johnson used to quip, you had best keep hidden in the kitchen. No one wants you to mention her, much less invite her to take tea in the parlor with the company. But there she is, rocking away in her chair by the stove.

Whatever the public response will be, before it is even encountered, there is one's own disappointment upon finishing a piece: the distance between the vision in the mind's eye of how it should look, or sound, or be and how it seems when complete. Elizabeth Bishop worked on her poem "The Moose" on and off for twenty years before she finally let it out of her hands to be published in *The New Yorker*. While many have rightly called it a masterpiece, it is still only twenty-eight six-line stanzas long, and it's easy to imagine her cursing herself for not being able to work it out to her own satisfaction years earlier and yet wanting to hold on to it longer, hoping to improve it more. Finishing poems and publishing them was terribly difficult for her. Even when she finally let them go, she often felt at best uncertain about them and at worse miserable and focused only on her sense that they had fallen short.

Indeed, her experience reminds us again of the way art-making and loss are so continually and profoundly intertwined. Finishing a work and taking it public may evoke in us a reminder of some essential loss. Writing about James Joyce, Marcel Proust, and Virginia Woolf, the psychoanalyst Alfred Margulies observed, "All were standing apart, disillusioned, alienated, and yet mourning the objects of their most naïve love, trying to recapture that which maybe never really was."[7] The search to recapture or re-create love already lost in time is always doomed to failure, even as it creates great art. And the old grief may return when you go public and are reminded that the audience you might unconsciously wish for is not the audience you will find. The artist seeks an actual contemporary audience. But, in part, he or she is often also simultaneously looking for the warm approval of those missing or long-dead eyes. The real and available gratification gets pinched by the tension between the contemporary reality and the wished-for reunion with past love, "which maybe never really was."

Furthermore, once public, you can no longer hide out in the fantasy of "How great it might be *if* I actually wrote down all the notes of that fabulous symphony that's been playing in my head for years." Once public, your work marks what you can do, and what you cannot, and it marks the real-time present.

I once tuned in to a radio interview with a playwright whose negative words offered good comfort. He allowed to his interlocutor that whenever he finished a play, he knew he was in for a rough time. However good it eventually turned out to be, for some weeks after he put down his pen, he just couldn't see any virtue in it. He felt certain it was inadequate and unperformable. No matter how many times he wrote successful plays, or how totally he understood that the feeling was as transitory as it was inevitable, it created a mental dissonance he could count on as part of his larger process of ending and letting go.

Not everyone reacts as he did—or like Bishop, or like folks for whom the loss is writ large—and even for him this reaction was temporary and part of a larger arc of feelings. Many are relieved; some thrilled; others mostly satisfied. And often people ricochet among a host of feelings: *This is the best work ever created—at least by me; it is the worst.* But the playwright's mood captures a common moment. As you go public, you peer at your effort with a new eye. Some people, or many people at some moments, squint, and feel satisfied, and see themselves reflected back in an evening gown or tuxedo, dressed for a night on the town. For others, or at other moments, the experience can be withering—like an encounter with the sickly florescent light that seems always to haunt women's dressing rooms in department stores; calculated to reflect back blotched skin, bulges, asymmetries, one's lesser features washed out and magnified.

Observing, and noting one of many fluctuations in his appraisal of his own work, Proust captured the way disappointment fills the distance between what is imagined and what is produced:

Those passages which, when I wrote them, were so co-
lourless in comparison with my thought, so complicated
and opaque in comparison with my harmonious and
transparent vision, so full of gaps which I had not man-
aged to fill, that the reading of them was a torture to me,
had only accentuated in me the sense of my own impo-
tence and of my incurable lack of talent.[8]

IF PROUST WAS obsessed with *his* lack of talent and *his* creative impotence, one wonders what the rest of us mortals are to do other than feel relieved that we're not alone in such worries. On the other hand, if he, too, feels such intense self-criticism, it also suggests we might take our own with a large grain of salt since the phenomenon is so widely shared among people who create.

V

I HAVE MET more than a few artists, painters, and writers who complete works but who simply cannot bear to go public. From what they say, they simply feel too vulnerable or too afraid of being criticized or of triggering deep shame. They may feel sty-mied by a perfectionist foreboding that their work will be found lacking, which, of course, is true. How could it not be? Who produces work that will not be found lacking on some fronts, no matter how much it delights on others? If such fears stopped everyone, there would be no art or craft ever shown or sold.

Sometimes, the choice not to go public is simply a way of avoiding the whole inevitable process of rejection, and of perhaps some trepidation that it will be unremitting. As a child living for a while in Vermont, I had as occasional babysitter a woman, by then in her late forties, who for decades had wanted badly to succeed as a writer, and who had gradually papered all four walls of her bathroom with rejection letters from hundreds of magazines. When you used her toilet, *The New Yorker*'s decorous, neatly printed stationery, bearing its correct and proper "No," met you square in the eye. Even as a child, I could feel her pain seeping through her wry effort to cope by posting the notes.

And while her tale captures many artists' worst fears, my sense is that it's something of an exception as real defeat goes. For each person who plays out the line as far as she can but still loses the fish, there are dozens who find it unbearable to face the sport's protracted, athletic reeling and unreeling. If the creature doesn't jump into the boat, or at least give up quickly, they consider the effort over and themselves dismissed. They don't find any pleasure in the strenuous nature of the outing. And then, some folks are purists. They won't flex their focus. If the striped bass isn't running, they refuse to bait for the more mundane mackerel.

I suspect that the single most common blunder those wishing to create art make is to assume that the fact that their work has been rejected—whether once or many times—offers unequivocal and incontrovertible evidence that it is inadequate for the market. But it isn't one market, it's many, and people often fail to grasp that ambiguity. The question comes down to whether this particular work is so poorly realized, or out of sync with the cultural moment, that no one will want it, or if it is it really good enough and just not well matched with the places you've tried, or for them at the moment you tried them.

Most beginning artists underestimate how hard it is to move a work into the public world, how much the victory favors persistence, and particularly a self-correcting persistence that takes in intelligent feedback offered along the way. If the rejections are endless, then you likely need to talk over your work and your situation with a more senior artist and to try to get a bead on what you may need to improve or alter. Or, you may just not quite be ready. Most artists produce plenty—by which I mean even decades—of early work that never finds any audience. Producing it allows them to learn their craft.

But overall, folks tend to be more aware of how the world does not hastily rush to their aid, less aware of how quickly rejections and criticisms may have caused them to turn tail long before any bugle actually sounds retreat. The more ways you can find to tolerate the process, the more likely you are to find your own way.

The poet Anne Sexton, as she began in the late 1950s trying to publish her poems, developed an approach that worked well, and that, once she became successful, she used to describe to young writers as a way to encourage them. Whenever she felt ready to send a poem out, she would make a list of twenty-five magazines to which she could send it. At the top of her list were the more prestigious and high-paying ones—*The New Yorker*, then *Harper's*, *The Atlantic*, and so on, with smaller, less well-known periodicals further toward the bottom of her list. She made a rule for herself that she would not mail a poem to the first magazine on the list without addressing the envelope for her second effort, and so on. So, if and when a rejection letter arrived, she could simply shove the next envelope into the mailbox. Should a particular poem fare really poorly, she would add a second set of twenty-five magazines to its list.

Not only did this practice keep her from losing heart when poems were rejected, it helped her remain optimistic about her prospects and progress. She'd look at her lists and see the names of the magazines, both the ones in which she'd already been published and the ones in which she hoped to get published, and remind herself of the progress she was making, and of her desire to have her work appear in the magazines at the top of her list. And, in time, it did.[9]

Online submission, while different in its physical labor, is no less daunting. The wall-papering rejection letters have often given way to silence, though occasionally you still get a form email or a personal response. More often, the unspoken code is "You'll hear from us if we want what you have." Still, the basis of Sexton's method remains sound. Somehow, each of us must find a strategy that lets us hang in as we send and resend our work, or approach galleries and juried shows, or audition for parts, or talk with wholesalers or managers at fairs or retail stores about selling what we've crafted.

Nor is getting the work out to a public the end of the challenge; another difficult surprise for many is the collective indifference to your work once it *is* out "there." You hang in a gallery, you publish a poem or a book, you record a new tune, or you set up your website to sell the quilts you've sewn. No one notices. Instead of the applause you hoped for, or the hisses you feared, you find that your overload of adrenaline, excitement, and angst is met with silence—with a void, with maybe a few hits on your website or an email from a loyal friend, but nothing more. Sometimes, this perception is simply the result of misunderstanding the time lag—the months and years of effort it sometimes takes for an audience to find your work. Other times, it is the whole experience. A year or so ago, I watched a first novel that had received a titanic advance drop like a stone into the silent deep. There were a few puff pieces before it was published, and some good reviews, but it didn't catch hold, and the publisher sadly swallowed its oversize investment and let the book die.

A colleague repeated to me a clever metaphor about publisher/author dilemmas told to her in her writing group. For a writer, she noted, producing a book is a mammalian process. There is a long gestation and often a painful birth, and one focuses with rapture, self-absorption, terror, and great emotional vulnerability upon the offspring's progress into the world. For a publisher, the birth is reptilian. It lays a bunch of eggs, turns its back, and waits with detachment to see which ones hatch and survive. No doubt publishers, and particularly the young publicists who work so frantically to market books, would find this view less than amusing and would likely view themselves as mammalian against a reptilian public. However . . . the metaphor certainly offers an apt version of a frequent feeling among writers about the larger reception of a work.

To complicate matters, a truly negative response to a work can signify a backhanded compliment. Some years ago, I had an "aha" moment on this score. Tom Wolfe had just published a novel. Both John Updike and Norman Mailer wrote reviews of it, and both tore it to shreds. At first I wondered why they would do that to another guy in their club—so to speak. When I thought about the phenomenon, I realized that the more accomplished you become, the more you draw powerful critics. The pinnacle of success is being shredded by an impressive beast rather than by a small rat. You are a great gladiator when you get eaten by a big literary lion. My small taste of this phenomenon, being shredded by the occasional midlevel jackal, does not reassure me that it's a positive experience in any way, but it may be as good as it sometimes gets. (On a similar note, the wife of a writer once said to me that her husband never read his reviews, but he never forgot who wrote them.)

The Wolfe story also demonstrates the obvious fact that success grants no immunity for subsequent works. If anything, the opposite is true. The collective psyche seems to favor a wheel of fortune, or at least a Ferris wheel approach, wherein people are allowed to rise, and then they fall, perhaps to return, or even rise further should they have stomach to stay aboard. But each level of success grants more notice—negative and positive.

Contemplating all the struggles of the effort, it's easy to see why some artists choose not to venture out. Even unusually talented ones may keep their work secret or at least private, and for diverse reasons. Gerard Manley Hopkins, for instance, found it torturous to try to reconcile the personal ambition manifest in publishing his poems with the self-renunciation he felt his devotion to God demanded. Though he'd published while a university student, once he became a priest he mostly denied himself that portion of the artist's life. And, on one occasion when he relented, his church stepped in and denied it to him.

For less clear reasons, the artist Hedda Sterne became increasingly reclusive as she aged. Sterne was the sole woman, or one of a very few, who could claim membership in the famous New York group of abstract expressionists, a gaggle that included such stars as Jackson Pollock, Mark Rothko, Robert Motherwell, and Willem de Kooning—among others. Sterne painted or drew for hours every day but eventually lost interest in partying and taking part in the art "scene." As she aged, she seemed to feel that it was only the doing of the work that compelled her. "Drawing," she told an interviewer when she was ninety-three years old, "is continuity. Everything else is interruption, even the night and sleep . . . I could die at any moment. But I still learn. Every drawing teaches me something."[10]

Opposite Sterne, there are those who, like Van Gogh, want desperately to find an audience and sell their art but die believing that their efforts have failed. (In truth, had Van Gogh not killed himself at thirty-seven, very likely his fame would have grown as quickly in his life as it did posthumously.) Similarly, Van Gogh's friend Paul Gauguin died at fifty-four, worn out not only by his own excesses but also by the dearth of public recognition for his work.

If you feel deeply conflicted about going public, perhaps the question becomes which discomfort you'd rather live with: a feeling that you might have tried, or tried harder, to get your work seen, but chose not to, and so sacrificed knowing what could have been possible; or the feeling that you did try, and most likely found some mix of satisfaction and disappointment. (Even when you have some success, you are likely to feel that by extending your arm and fingers as far as possible, you can almost touch the next level of larger renown, and the opportunities it offers, but can only grasp something smaller and more local. A feeling perhaps as old as cultures and striving, but, thanks to global markets, now even more common.) Yes, collective attention tends to focus in a few bright beams that light the night sky. Yet, if you choose not to try, you leave your lamp unlit and never learn fully about the space it might illuminate.

coda

ONE NIGHT AT dinner, an old friend, a writer, was musing over his own life and recollecting how he had changed from a boy indifferent to books to an adolescent so in their thrall that by the time he finished a stint in the army and entered a university, he knew he had to become a poet. Fifty years later he easily recalled precisely the moment the transformation began. He was in tenth grade, athletic, someone who enjoyed the hockey rink more than the classroom, beer and a cigarette more than a pen. His English teacher had assigned the opening chapter of *Heart of Darkness*. He lay in his bunk in his dormitory room and tried to read it, but he found it impenetrable. The sentences were dense and senseless. Who cared where they led?

Completely frustrated, he hurled the paperback across the room. But, still, he mused, he liked his English teacher. And he knew there'd be questions about the text in class the next day. So, a while later, he retrieved the volume and began to read again.

This time, something clicked; who knows what. Perhaps a critical bunch of synapses linked up; certainly his hormones must have been flowing. I suspect his heart was involved, though the "heart" I refer to, like its counterpart "the mind," is the metaphoric one, also located partly within the confines of his skull, partly throughout his body. I mention heart because I imagine his good feelings toward his teacher, and perhaps a slight apprehension about displeasing him, may have offered him just enough encouragement to keep at the book, to entertain a bit of curiosity as to what this particular, onerous pile of pages was about.

What he remembered so many years later was that when he returned to reading *Heart of Darkness*, the words suddenly stopped perplexing him, and he read the story through, gripped, moved, and captivated. Needless to say, after this book, he found the next one, and on and on so that now his bookshelves are stuffed full of carefully chosen volumes.[1]

A sentimental tale? Perhaps in the current public world where intellectual excitement is often devalued, if not treated with contempt. Many would declare that such a narrative of literary discovery is now a tale out of time, vestigial, or at least dulled by being too often told. While the passion for stories is universal, the need to read them, some argue, is less relevant than it might have been one hundred years ago—before movies, television, Internet. But, if you have experienced some similar transformation about the written word, you cannot help but hold his tale dear. And perhaps more so because it *is* so common. (In *The*

Uncommon Reader, Alan Bennett imagines Queen Elizabeth's mental life transforming as she immerses herself in books, and the novel jests delightfully about this kind of awakening.)² To me, the poet's recollection feels like a completely familiar and yet completely mysterious life-changing moment, one encountered regularly by new generations of readers. And it is at once similar to and different from my own "awakening" to art, which, forty-some years later, has led me on this errand. Oh yes, of course, my family, my friends, my psychotherapy work are essential, but along with them, living as a serious amateur, an appreciator, and an apprentice—spending free time taken up with books, films, painting, music, and ideas—has also felt essential. Not long ago, I observed to a colleague that one always wastes one's life. How can we do otherwise when time is relentless, and as E. M. Forster once observed, we are performing on stage even as we are learning the instrument on which we perform? Yet I have been pleased to waste mine in this fashion.

I can feel bored to death in museums when I'd rather be catching up with friends. Sometimes reading gets reduced to dull habit, and I finish a book out of obligation rather than desire. But any lover of food sometimes feels the same way about dinner. You can save for months for a high-end meal, only to leave feeling indifferent. Yet, appetite sharp, you can meet up with just the right plate of eggs and home fries in an unlikely dive and savor every bite. In a similar vein, I went kicking and protesting to the theater recently, reluctant to sit through another Shakespeare play with my English teacher husband and his endless appetite for Shakespeare plays, only to find myself completely caught up in an unlikely, strange, funny production of *Titus Andronicus*. Or, as an older friend observed more generally, "I will stay alive as long as I can just to encounter the next surprise, the next unforeseen happening."

The poet became first a reader and then eventually a writer, and his awakening to books is an obvious antecedent to his wish to write. Each experience may have a different cast, but writers are not so dissimilar in their motives from readers. At least in my case, as a nonfiction writer and essayist, the difference is in emphasis. I write first to understand what I'm feeling and thinking about something, and then to try to narrate it in a way that engages others. But the point I'm trying to capture vis-à-vis a reader's awakening is that it constitutes most simply a sense of deep excitement about a possibility, in part real, in part an illusion—maybe an illusion that one can quell the chaos and finally get it (whatever "it" is). Or, more realistically, that we can understand a little more, or feel a little less alone, or leave our troubles behind for a while, or just enjoy vicariously something forbidden or beyond our reach.

Additionally, a reader may grasp that a writer has described thoughts and feelings, some that he possesses, some that feel alien, but that were previously unnamed or unreflected so acutely in his own inner world. And that process answers a question held within him, but perhaps not consciously known, and it confirms something ineffable. I recall reluctantly reading some of Samuel Johnson's writings for a college class and maybe an hour into the assigned texts realizing that in encountering this quirky, tic-plagued weirdo 200 years dead, I'd linked up with a wry, sympathetic sensibility who not only amused me but also made me feel less alone and strangely sane.

Books are probes sent into deep space, seeking other sentient life; readers are the sentinels watching the night sky, like huge radar complexes, but with eyes and ears and feelings. Readers seek the probes, seek what's *sympathique*, alive, novel, entertaining, informing, baroque, and strange in others' sensibilities; readers, of course, also seek answers particular and cosmic.

Often, I suspect, the artist's awakening follows an arc from passionate pleasure, to identification with those who have created it, and a wish to become a creator. The more immersed you become in the melodies, the more you want to play along. Giuseppe Tomasi di Lampedusa, the reclusive, very odd Sicilian aristocrat who wrote *The Leopard*—one of the greatest Italian novels of the last century, and a huge best seller—began work on it, his first and only novel, at age fifty-eight, and failed at his attempt to publish the work before he died two years later. He had no experience writing fiction when he undertook the project. But he'd spent his entire life reading, and had read more literature in more languages than the rest of us likely have had opportunity to read in our own. (He only rarely pursued paid work, and his daily ritual was to spend time in secondhand bookstores finding books and in cafés drinking coffee and reading them.) When he exhausted Italian, English, French, German, and Russian literature, he taught himself Spanish so as to have fresh works to savor. And when he loved a book, he sometimes read it many times. I suspect his process of mastering writing occurred in his mind, as he pondered and analyzed others' efforts. After absorbing so much literature, it seems he felt impelled and ready to create his own.[3]

Meanwhile, a telltale in people who have not yet found their work is the quiet sadness that haunts them, whether they know its source consciously or not. They need to pursue the kind of absorbing errand I have described, but they have not yet found a way. Leaving home may feel too difficult, and certainly impractical. But they are also paying a price for resisting that inconvenience. Their desire may bury itself under all the days' duties and obligations and other interests. It may go dormant, but it lingers. I was talking not long ago to a young doctor who had been a serious musician before medical school. She'd started playing as a child and pursued it through school until the demands of her training overwhelmed her and her living situation deprived her of adequate time and private physical space. She'd dropped by my office to follow up a brief hall conversation. We didn't have long. But, curious, I asked her how it was for her not to be playing. And before she could think to respond, tears started rolling down her cheeks.

Her spontaneous sorrow reminded me of an evening maybe twenty-five years ago when I attended a party for a writer. I knew the host, but none of the other guests, and my decision to attend, alone, on a weeknight after work, was unlike me. (My sons were little, and I hated leaving them at night if I'd already been away to work.) It had been years since I'd been among so many writers, and hearing chatter about their efforts and undertakings struck a deep chord. I only stayed briefly and was surprised as I drove home to find unexpected tears on my own cheeks. I had spent years assuring myself that writing would be a wrong turn for me, and that I was much better off without it. Except that I wasn't. The longing, allowed into awareness, provided the clarity and incentive to commence the work of mastery. I remembered having read how Edward Albee gave himself play-writing as a birthday present, and I decided to imitate him in this particular way.

People's experiences are varied. I asked a sculptor friend what she recalled about how she came to sculpt. She wrote this response, and it seems to me to capture well how one's psyche and an exposure to a relevant medium can come together:

I don't believe there was a precise moment when I knew I wanted to become an artist. I believe I just grew into it. I don't think my talent propelled me as much as an active imagination and the desire to live in its domain. Our household as I was growing up was noisy and boisterous. My older brothers and I were constantly battling for our positions within the family. More often than not I was overpowered in these struggles. The one place I had control over my environment was in my room. I had an incredible number of dolls and stuffed animals. I created a kingdom (or rather queendom) complete with a social structure. I was constantly rearranging the room to accommodate the give and take of this make-believe society. What gave me the most pleasure was creating a spatial/visual world—I would spend hours making the room "feel" right and would then sit on my bed looking with awe at my handy work. My room was my ultimate refuge and was also where I was able to recapture myself and find meaning within a fairly chaotic household.

We also lived within a few blocks of a wonderful art museum where I started taking art classes at age five. I remember the teachers using my constructions to show as examples to the other students. This of course gave me a ready audience and boosted my confidence in something I was already keen about. Also by age eight my parents allowed me to walk to the museum by myself and I remember spending what seemed like hours wandering in the Egyptian, Greek, and Asian sculpture and architecture rooms in complete rapture—my imagination spinning.

When I was about fourteen my father gave me two monographs on the sculptors Louise Nevelson and David Smith. I remember being overcome with emotion when I first saw their work in person. I think it was at this point that I realized that one could make a life as an artist. What is curious to me however is that it was only when I had finished college that I had the courage to tell my parents and myself that I was going to be an artist.[4]

I WROTE TO a musician friend to ask him about his own experience, and his response was unequivocal and dramatic and describes the way some people know very early what they are about. (Similarly, I remember reading in Edith Wharton's memoir, *A Backward Glance*, that from the time she was only a few years old, she would start holding books in her lap, pretending to read them, and making up stories. And that she became a writer as a very young child.) The musician states:

The true musician responds to an inner necessity, his calling, his "elective affinity," to employ Goethe's term, and usually responds right away, practically at birth. When as a teenager I first played [piano] for Nadia Boulanger, my mentor for many years and well beyond those, she said, after hearing a mere four measures of a Beethoven sonata, "You are a born musician!" This miraculous woman, above and beyond her extraordinary powers as both musician and pedagogue, had an unfailing radar-like receptivity to what was real or ersatz, so it would be needless to insist on how much her acceptance meant to me.[5]

...G ABOUT THESE friends, I found myself thinking about L.. on's very relevant line "The whole secret of a teacher's force is that men are convertible. They want awakening." I long ago scribbled down this notion of his, and it has stayed with me. A teacher's force. Each speaker's narrative somewhere mentions a teacher who mirrored back to him or her something important. Perhaps fondness, perhaps a recognition of his worth or her talent. Something intimate happened, together with something abstract, cerebral, aesthetic. When you encounter the work, the sculptures of Nevelson, the music of Beethoven or John Cage, the stories of Joseph Conrad, you are moved. But you are not alone. You are moved and somewhere there is someone, often a teacher or mentor, who is with you in your mind.

I initially came to reading seriously as a way to hold my father's interest since it was clear that he had no time to share pleasures I possessed that deviated from his own creative urgencies. Both my parents were constant readers. But for a long time the world of books was theirs, and while it carried me in its current, it did not begin to be mine until I took a class in high school about the Romantic poets. Then, at fifteen and sixteen, I started reading and rereading the verses and, blown away, became a convert. In spring we read Wordsworth, and our teacher made a small pedagogic gesture that was life-changing for me. He suggested that we could write a term paper about the poems we were reading, or we could memorize ten of them chosen by him. Sick of writing papers, I memorized the assigned lines of

"Tintern Abbey," "Nuns Fret Not" and other sonnets, a verse of "The Prelude," and the daffodil poem here used in chapter 5, "I Wandered Lonely as a Cloud." One grade school teacher in a Vermont public school had insisted we memorize the Twenty-Third Psalm, and later, our ninth-grade teacher had assigned the first sing-song stanzas of Longfellow's *Evangeline*. But this later high school assignment hit home. I discovered that carrying other people's rhyme and meter in my mind expanded it and pleased me. The poems worked on me like some lamplighter making his way at dusk, streetlamp to streetlamp, around a large square. I could sit in the café, aperitif in hand, elated, still, contemplating them all aglow.

In the summer after school was out, I read Walter Jackson Bate's biography of Keats, and I memorized a handful of Keats's sonnets including "When I Have Fears" described in chapter 2. I stopped memorizing in my late forties because, though phrases had always had a way of breaking loose and rearranging themselves in my mind, the effort gradually yielded too little. Mostly now I possess lines and fragments that float peaceably and surface as different feelings and memories cue them. But the poems I memorized as a teenager and young adult became the wall struts of my mental room, and they became a standard—unreachable yet worth pursuing—of how to write. They taught me the value of condensation and tight language, and they provided the cadences that have led me along. I used to joke that poems are the prayers of the irreverent, and certainly mine have kept me company offering the comfort of solidarity without heavy-handed instruction.

This book, I knew preconsciously along the way but realize more fully now, has held a second story within its primary effort to describe something about the potential obstacles in mastering art-making. It has also constituted an effort to revisit and speak about some of the exposures to artists and art—some mainstream, others more quirky—that moved me deeply when I was young, and that informed me. Books, photographs, movies, music, painting, and sculpture, along with the people I've loved who've helped me comprehend them, have furnished my mind and sustained me. They also infected me with the unbearable but inescapable wish to attempt to hum along with their greater music, to take on my own fears, and to agree to undertake the long, fraught, satisfying apprenticeship of trying to master a form. Like Bunyan's pilgrim, I have arrived at a city, but unlike his, mine is earthbound, a psychological space in which I have had the good fortune to find ways to bear the anxiety of effort.

ACKNOWLEDGEMENTS

I THANK MIRIAM ALTSHULER, for her wonderful, dedicated agenting and warm personal support. I thank Michael T. Gilmore, Margaret Stark, Robb Forman Dew, Alfred Margulies, Wendy Lesser, and David Smith for generously and thoughtfully reading chapters and earlier drafts of this book. At Counterpoint Press, I thank my editor, Dan Smetanka, for grasping my intent and knowing how to nudge the text along. I thank Mikayla Butchart for her careful copyediting; and Kelly Winton, and everyone else at Counterpoint who worked to produce and market the book. I thank, too, the many friends, colleagues, patients, and supervisees who have helped me understand how they viewed their own creative efforts and their dilemmas making art. I thank Zack Smith and Peter Smith for their conversations with me about their music-making, and I further thank Peter for his generous editing assists. Finally, I want to express gratitude to Leston Havens (1924–2011), a psychiatrist, professor, independent thinker, and encouraging mentor and colleague. Les was a man of erudition and sly wit whose fierce belief in enabling psychological freedom guided his psychotherapeutic work, his writing, and his teaching. His perspective lives on in many minds, including my own.

NOTES

CHAPTER 1

1 Bill Buford, *Heat* (New York: Vintage Books, 2006), 111.

2 Gary Miranda, *Listeners at the Breathing Place* (Princeton, NJ: Princeton University Press, 1978).

3 Edward P. Jones, *The Known World* (New York: Amistad, 2003), 2.

4 Richard Wilbur, "Love Calls Us to the Things of This World," in *The Poems of Richard Wilbur* (New York: Harcourt, Brace and World, 1963), 65–66.

5 David Denby, review of *To Be and to Have*, directed by Nicolas Philibert, *The New Yorker*, October 6, 2003, http://www.newyorker.com/arts/reviews/film/to_be_and_to_have_philibert.

6 Jonathan Lear, *Radical Hope: Ethics in the Face of Cultural Devastation* (Cambridge, MA: Harvard University Press, 2006), 119.

7 Anne Sexton, "The Freak Show," in *Written in Water, Written in Stone: Twenty Years of Poets on Poetry*, ed. Martin Lammon (Ann Arbor, MI: University of Michigan Press, 1997), 217.

8 Studs Terkel, *Working: People Talk about What They Do All Day and How They Feel about What They Do* (New York: Pantheon, 1974), xiv.

9   Erich Auerbach, *Mimesis: The Representation of Reality in Western Literature* (Princeton, NJ: Princeton University Press, 1953), 350.

10   Henry James, *Roderick Hudson* (1875; New York: Penguin Classics, 1986), 53.

CHAPTER 2

1   Walter Jackson Bate, *John Keats* (New York: Oxford University Press, 1966), 292.

2   Leston Havens, *Coming to Life* (Cambridge, MA: Harvard University Press, 1993), 165–66.

3   Wilbur, "Love Calls Us to the Things of This World" (see chap. 1, n. 4).

4   Julian Barnes, *Nothing to Be Frightened Of* (New York: Alfred A. Knopf, 2008), 27.

5   Robert Kegan, *In over Our Heads: The Mental Demands of Modern Life* (Cambridge, MA: Harvard University Press, 1994), 265; Janna Malamud Smith, "Walking to Wisconsin," in *Voices: The Art and Science of Psychotherapy* 45, no. 1 (spring 2009): 58–64.

6   Rainer Maria Rilke, *Letters on Cézanne* (New York: Fromm International Publishing Corp., 1985), 86.

7   Miranda, *Listeners at the Breathing Place*, 41 (see chap. 1, n. 2).

8   Erica E. Hirshler, *Sargent's Daughters: The Biography of a Painter* (Boston: MFA Publications, 2009), 18; E. B. White quoted by Roger Angell, "Andy," in *The New Yorker*, February 14 and 21, 2005, p. 142.

9   Marcel Proust, *Swann's Way*, trans. C. K. Scott Moncrieff (London: Chatto & Windus, 1957), 10–11.

10   Bate, *John Keats*, 292.

CHAPTER 3

1 Abe Frajndlich, *Lives I've Never Lived: A Portrait of Minor White* (Cleveland: Arc Press, 1983), 45.

2 David Gates, "Restless Imagination," review of *Charles Dickens: A Life*, by Claire Tomalin, and *Becoming Dickens: The Invention of a Novelist*, by Robert Douglas-Fairhurst, *The New York Times Book Review*, November 6, 2011, 8.

3 "Thriller," recorded by Michael Jackson, composed by Rod Temperton, 1984, Epic, lyrics available online at Elyrics.net, http://www.elyrics.net/read/m/michael-jackson-lyrics/thriller-lyrics.html; for a good summary description of Joe Jackson's abuse of Michael, see Margo Jefferson, *On Michael Jackson* (New York: Vintage Books, 2006), 33–37.

4 "Dave," Best Answer to Resolved Question, "How exactly was michael jackson abused by his father and why?" Yahoo! Answers, 2009, http://answers.yahoo.com/question/index?qid=20090627152807AAVmHiO.

5 D. W. Winnicott, "Transitional objects and transitional phenomena," in *Through Paediatrics to Psycho-Analysis: Collected Papers* (New York: Basic Books, Inc., 1975), 230–31.

6 Ursula K. LeGuin, "Talking about Writing," in *The Language of the Night: Essays on Fantasy and Science Fiction* (New York: Penguin Group, 1979), 195.

CHAPTER 4

1 X. J. Kennedy, "Poets," in *Cross Ties: Selected Poems* (Athens, GA: University of Georgia Press, 1985), 49.

2 Renée Fleming, *The Inner Voice: The Making of a Singer* (New York: Penguin, 2004), 103.

3 John Marchese, *The Violin Maker* (New York: HarperCollins, 2007), 20–21.

4   J. L. Herman, "Craft and Science in the Treatment of Traumatized People," *Journal of Trauma & Dissociation* 9, no. 3 (2008): 293–300.

5   I first explored this Havelock Ellis story in my book *Private Matters: In Defense of the Personal Life* (New York: Addison Wesley, 1997), 132. Ellis tells the story in *Studies in the Psychology of Sex: The Evolution of Modesty, the Phenomenon of Sexual Periodicity, and Auto-Eroticism* (Philadelphia: F. A. Davis Company, 1901), 44.

6   Charles Chaplin, *My Autobiography* (New York: Penguin Books, 1966), 23 and 26.

7   Ibid., 17–18.

CHAPTER 5

1   This moment is recounted both in Frances Wilson's *The Ballad of Dorothy Wordsworth* (New York: Farrar, Straus and Giroux, 2009), 176–77, and in Adam Sisman's *The Friendship: Wordsworth and Coleridge* (New York: Penguin, 2006), 345–46.

2   D. W. Winnicott, "The Capacity to Be Alone (1958)," in *The Maturational Processes and the Facilitating Environment: Studies in Theory of Emotional Development*, ed. John D. Sutherland (London: Hogarth Press and Institute of Psycho-Analysis, 1976), 29–36.

3   Sisman, *The Friendship*, 53.

4   Stephen Gill, *William Wordsworth: A Life* (New York: Oxford University Press, 1999), 202–3; Wilson, *Ballad*, 180–5.

5   Ibid., 17.

6   Ibid., 275.

7   Evan Hughes, "Just Kids," *New York Magazine*, October 9, 2011, http://nymag.com/arts/books/features/jeffrey-eugenides-2011-10.

8   Brandon Keim, "Power of Mom's Voice Silenced by Instant Messages," *Wired*, January 5, 2012, http://www.wired.com/wiredscience/2012/01/instant-messaging-stress.

9   "Infectious Health Behaviors," *Harvard Mental Health Letter*, August 2009, 6.

10 For a fuller account of contemporary loneliness, see Jacqueline Olds and Richard Schwartz, *The Lonely American* (Boston: Beacon Press, 2009).

CHAPTER 6

1   Dan Chiasson, "Works on Paper: The Letters of Elizabeth Bishop and Robert Lowell," *The New Yorker*, November 3, 2008, http://www.new yorker.com/arts/critics/books/2008/11/03/081103crbo_books_chiasson.

2   Thomas Travisano with Saskia Hamilton, eds., *Words in Air: The Complete Correspondence between Elizabeth Bishop and Robert Lowell* (New York: Farrar, Straus and Giroux, 2008), 136. In my book *Private Matters*, in a chapter entitled "Burnt Letters, Biography, and Privacy" (145–72), I discuss artists' letters from another angle.

3   *Words in Air*, July 2, 1948, 41.

4   Ibid., 279.

5   Ibid., July 27, 1960, 332.

6   Ibid., July 12, 1960, 331.

7   Ibid., June 27, 1961, 366; August 7, 1961, 369; June 15, 1964, 543.

8   Diane Wood Middlebrook, *Anne Sexton* (Boston: Houghton Mifflin, 1991), 142.

9   *Words in Air*, January 1, 1954, 151.

10 Ibid., 175 and 369.

11 Ibid., 494.

12 Ibid., August 9, 1957, 213; August 15, 1957, 219.

13 Ibid., August 15, 1957, 225–26.

14 Ibid., August 28, 1957, 229.

15   Wikipedia, s.v. "George Sand," last modified March 5, 2012, http://
     en.wikipedia.org/wiki/George_Sand.

16   I am no longer sure where I read the Boissevain quotation. But I've
     found it footnoted by another writer as appearing in Daniel Mark
     Epstein, *What Lips My Lips Have Kissed: The Loves and Love Poems of
     Edna St. Vincent Millay* (New York: Henry Holt, 2001), 182.

17   Marcel Proust, *The Captive* in *The Captive & The Fugitive, In Search
     of Lost Time*, vol. 5, paperback ed., trans. C. K. Scott Moncrieff and
     Terence Kilmartin, rev. D. J. Enright (New York: Modern Library,
     2003), 239–40.

18   Alfred Habegger, *My Wars Are Laid Away in Books: The Life of Emily
     Dickinson* (New York: Random House, 2001), 131.

19   Thomas Bulfinch, "Orpheus and Eurydice" in *Stories of Gods and
     Heroes, Bulfinch's Mythology, Classic Reader*, http://www.classicreader.
     com/book/2823/26/.

20   *Words in Air*, 797.

CHAPTER 7

1   Thomas Hardy, *Jude the Obscure* (1895; New York: Signet Classic,
     1961), 68.

2   Hirsher, *Sargent's Daughters*, 54 (see chap. 2, n. 8).

3   "Daughter Auctions Stradivari Cello to Hear It Again," *Weekend
     Edition Sunday*, NPR, January 15, 2012, radio broadcast, http://www
     .npr.org/2012/01/15/145259558/daughter-auctions-stradivari-cello
     -to-hear-it-again.

4   Musa Mayer, *Night Studio: A Memoir of Philip Guston* (Cambridge: Da
     Capo Press, 1997), 10–13.

5   Ibid., 50.

6   Ibid., 34–35.

7   Ibid., 39 and 41.

8 Ibid., 40.

9 Sue Halpern, "Who Was Steve Jobs," review of *Steve Jobs*, by Walter Isaacson, Simon and Schuster, *The New York Review of Books*, January 12, 2012, http://www.nybooks.com/articles/archives/2012/jan/12/who-was-steve-jobs.

10 Alan Bennett, *The Habit of Art* (London: Faber and Faber Limited, 2009), ix; Edna O'Brien, *James Joyce* (New York: Penguin/Viking, 1999), 129.

11 Martin Eisendstadt and Dean Keith Simonton are two whose work is described by Daniel Coyle in *The Talent Code* (New York: Bantam Books, 2009), 112–14.

12 Jurgen Trimborn, *Leni Riefenstahl: A Life* (New York: Faber and Faber, 2002), 252; see also the film *The Wonderful, Horrible Life of Leni Riefenstahl*, directed by Ray Müller, 1993; see also Susan Sontag, "Fascinating Fascism," review of *The Last of the Nuba* by Leni Riefenstahl (New York: Harper & Row), and *SS Regalia* by Jack Pia (Ballantine Books), *The New York Review of Books*, February 6, 1975, http://www.nybooks.com/articles/archives/1975/feb/06/fascinating-fascism.

13 Lady Gaga, "Marry the Night" official video, YouTube video, 13:51, posted by "LadyGagaVEVO," December 2, 2011, http://www.youtube.com/watch?v=cggNqDAtJYU.

14 Lady Gaga, "Judas" official video, YouTube video, 5:35, posted by "LadyGagaVEVO," May 3, 2011, http://www.youtube.com/watch?v=wagn8Wrmzuc&ob=av2.

15 "Lady Gaga Shares Everything," *The Ellen Degeneres Show*, YouTube video, 6:41, posted by "TheEllenShow," January 11, 2011, http://www.youtube.com/watch?NR=1&v=NOpSC9F04IU&feature=endscreen.

16 "Lady Gaga talks about being bullied on 'The View,'" *The View*, YouTube video, 0:40, posted by "Monstermiley92," June 4, 2011, http://www.youtube.com/watch?v=-3QO2DCmh9M&feature=related.

17 "Lady Gaga on Oprah Interview Part 1! (01/1510)," *Oprah*, YouTube video, 6:08, posted by "JuiceBox448," January 17, 2010, http://www.youtube.com/watch?v=d3f2duc7oyw; see also Lisa Robinson, "Lady

Gaga, a Wild and Candid (What Did You Expect) Interview," *Vanity Fair* (January 2012), 50–113.

18 "Lady Gaga: Behind the '60 Minutes' Interview," *60 Minutes*, 60 Minutes Overtime, CBSNews online, February 13, 2011, http://www.cbsnews.com/8301-504803_162-20031573-10391709.html?tag=segmentExtraScroller;housing.

19 Janet Malcolm, *The Journalist and the Murderer* (New York: Vintage Books, 1990), 32–33. Janet Malcolm quotes Joe McGinness quoting Thomas Mann as quoted by Joseph Campbell.

20 Mayer, *Night Studio*, 99.

21 Lillian Hellman, *Pentimento* (Boston: Little Brown & Co., 1973), 278.

CHAPTER 8

1 Brett C. Millier, *Elizabeth Bishop: Life and the Memory of It* (Berkeley, CA: University of California Press, 1993), 284.

2 Todd Leopold, "The success of failure: Pulitzer Winner's surprising road to the top," CNN Living, January 28, 2012, http://www.cnn.com/2012/01/20/living/jennifer-egan-creativity-failure/index.html.

3 Jonathan Galassi et al, "A Symposium on Editing," *The Threepenny Review* 113, spring 2008, 16.

4 Anne Trubek, "Why Authors Tweet," *The New York Times Sunday Book Review*, January 8, 2012, 31.

5 Jon Pareles, "A Grizzled Troubadour Dusts Off His Bowler," *The New York Times*, October 20, 2011, http://www.nytimes.com/2011/10/23/arts/music/tom-waitss-new-album-bad-as-me.html?_r=2&pagewanted=all.

6 "Walt Whitman and Ralph Waldo Emerson," The Classroom Electric: Dickinson, Whitman, and American Culture, May 8, 2012, http://www.classroomelectric.org/volume1/belasco/whitman-emerson.htm.

7 Alfred Margulies, moderator, in introduction to Leonard Shengold's "Haunted by Parents—Virgina Woolf" (paper presented at Psychoanalytic Society of New England, East; Macht Auditorium, Cambridge Hospital; Cambridge, MA; December 5, 2009).

8 Marcel Proust, *The Fugitive*, in *The Captive* & *The Fugitive, In Search of Lost Time*, vol. 5, paperback ed., trans. C. K. Scott Moncrieff and Terence Kilmartin, rev. D. J. Enright (New York: Modern Library, 2003), 770.

9 Lois Ames, personal communication, December 2010.

10 Sarah Boxer, "Hedda Sterne: The Last Irascible," *The New York Review of Books*, December 23, 2010, 45.

CHAPTER 9

1 R.D., personal communication, October 2009.

2 Alan Bennett, *The Uncommon Reader* (New York: Farrar, Straus and Giroux, 2007).

3 David Gilmour, *The Last Leopard: The Life of Giuseppe Tomasi di Lampedusa* (New York: Pantheon Books, 1988).

4 M.S., personal communication, July 26, 2008.

5 J.G., personal communication, July 2008.

INDEX